The Rise of Biblical Criticism
in America, 1800–1870
THE NEW ENGLAND SCHOLARS

The Rise of Biblical Criticism

in America, 1800-1870

THE NEW ENGLAND SCHOLARS

BY

JERRY WAYNE BROWN

WESLEYAN UNIVERSITY PRESS

Middletown, Connecticut

Library of Congress Catalog Card Number: 69-17793

Manufactured in the United States of America

FIRST EDITION

CONTENTS

The Rise of Biblical Criticism
in America, 1800–1870
THE NEW ENGLAND SCHOLARS

INTRODUCTION

THE Bible is an ancient book: parts of it are almost 3000 years old, and even the most recent books of the New Testament were written 1800 years ago. Yet throughout the history of Christianity the Bible has been accepted as a normative source of belief and action. The relation of so old a literature to later historical periods creates certain problems. For example, in what sense can a twentieth-century religious community refer to the Book of Genesis as normative for its thought and action when that book arose 3000 years ago out of a culture with problems and modes of thought so different from those of the present?

Throughout the history of Christianity the fixed traditions of the Bible have been related to the changing traditions and problems of the church by means of interpretation. *Hermeneutics* is the technical term used to designate the discipline, or method, of interpretation.[1]

Even within the New Testament the problem of hermeneutics is clearly evident, particularly in the way the author of Matthew interprets the Hebrew scriptures for his own purposes.[2] Perhaps the first self-conscious system of hermeneutics within the church is that of the "Alexandria School." The outstanding figure of this movement was Origen, the third-century Christian scholar, who, however, was greatly influenced by Philo, the first-century Jewish commenta-

---

[1] For a general discussion of the history of hermeneutics, see Frederick W. Farrar, *History of Interpretation* (London: Macmillan, 1886).

[2] See Krister Stendahl, *The School of St. Matthew* (Uppsala: C. W. K. Gleerup, Lund, 1954).

tor. Both Philo and Origen introduced extensive allegorical exegesis
into their biblical studies. By means of allegory Philo had been able
both to reconcile Judaism with Hellenistic philosophy and to circum-
vent apparently contradictory statements. Origen did not hesitate to
state that the Bible contained many unhistorical and literally false
statements. The wise interpreter sought the symbolic truths within
narratives like the creation story and among contradictory accounts
of the life of Jesus in the Gospels. Nevertheless, while allegorical
interpretation freed the church from simple literalism, there was no
programmatic way of controlling the extent to which allegory might
be used.

By the beginning of the fourth century it had been recognized
that allowing everyone to interpret scripture would lead to theological chaos, and so it was commonly accepted that biblical interpretation should be the privilege of the Catholic church. The Bible
had been given to the church, it was argued, and consequently it
should be interpreted by those who stood within the apostolic succession. There existed a great flexibility within these confines, but
the flexibility was bounded by the complementarity of Catholic
interpretation and Catholic theology: although Catholic theology
was drawn from the Bible, modes of interpretation had to express
what had been believed "everywhere, always, by everyone."

The elasticity of biblical interpretation during the Middle Ages
was expressed by the commonly held notion that every text was to
be interpreted on various levels of meaning.[3] In verse, this notion
was expressed:

> The letter shows us what God and our Fathers did;
> The allegory shows us where our faith is hid;
> The moral meaning gives us rules of daily life;
> The anagogy shows us where we end our strife.[4]

In Galatians 4:22 ff., for example, the reference to Jerusalem may
be understood literally as a geographic location, but allegorically it

---

[3] On the interpretation of the Bible in the Middle Ages see Beryl Smalley,
The Study of the Bible in the Middle Ages (Oxford: Clarendon Press, 1941).

[4] Quoted in Robert M. Grant, *The Bible in the Church* (New York:
Macmillan, 1948), p. 101.

may be taken as the church, morally as the human soul, and anagogically, or mystically, as the heavenly city.

Exegesis during the Middle Ages was in no way rigid, since interpreters might seek as many as seven levels of meaning in a text or limit themselves to two or three. Furthermore, the scholar might tend to emphasize the importance of one meaning above others, as Thomas Aquinas tended to emphasize the literal sense of a text. However, in all cases hermeneutics was defined within the limits of Catholic theology.

The reformers of the sixteenth century sought to free the Bible from the interpretative traditions of the church so that it might address the individual directly. Although Calvin and Luther frequently referred to patristic exegesis and emphasized the literal, historical, and grammatical interpretation of the text, both were concerned to use the Bible as a judge of the church. Both Luther's Christocentrism and Calvin's systematic theology exercised great control over the process of exegesis but allowed some use of allegorical and typological interpretation.

Seventeenth-century Protestantism held a much more rigid view of the Bible and its interpretation. Whereas Calvin and Luther had, in principle at least, distinguished between the Word of God and the literal text of the Bible, later Protestants feared the dangers of subjective interpretation. They did not think of the Holy Spirit as working through the interpreter to transform the literal words of the Bible into the Word of God, but rather as inspiring the very writing of the books of the Bible. Thus they developed the doctrines of inspiration and infallibility. Instead of the Bible speaking to the Spirit-quickened heart of man, the Bible became the hard, infallible "stuff" of which dogmatic systems were made. Biblical interpretation moved within these confines and within particular dogmatic systems. The Bible was to be used as a source for "proof texts."

Protestants in New England, most notably the Puritans, adhered to a seventeenth-century view of biblical interpretation. However, the Puritan view of the inspiration and infallibility of the Bible was tempered by a strong strain of piety. The Puritan was not only concerned with right thinking, he was even more concerned with right acting. Puritan theology became an experienced theology that rejoiced in the omnipotent glory of an inscrutable God. Theological movements, and hence systems of biblical interpretation, tended to center around the experience of theology rather than methods of doing theology. But in the main Puritan exegesis consisted of proof-texting within confessional positions. Even the pre-Unitarian liberalism of men like Charles Chauncy and Jonathan Mayhew employed this general method, although without the traditional confessional position.[5]

American deism brought to the Bible its own sceptical point of view. However the deists stood outside the realm of church life, and men like Paine and Jefferson, while doubting the validity of biblical revelation, brought no significant critical and methodical techniques to bear on the Bible.

Significant innovations in the interpretation of the Bible were beginning to be felt in Europe as early as the seventeenth century. In France scholars had inaugurated the textual study of the Bible, recognizing that the biblical text in Hebrew and Greek had not been preserved intact. The English philosopher Thomas Hobbes declared that responsible study of the Bible should include proper dating of the various writings through careful comparison of traditional opinions. He suggested that much of the Old Testament had been written after the Exile and that Moses could not have written all of Deuteronomy. The Jewish philosopher Baruch Spinoza, who argued for free critical examination of the Scriptures, described the corpus of writings from Genesis to II Kings as a work composed of various contradictory elements compiled by the scribe Ezra. The French priest Richard Simon concurred with Spinoza, and in his *Histoire critique du Vieux Testament* (1678) provided the first critical introduction to the Old Testament.[6]

Notable advances in biblical study were made in the eighteenth century on numerous fronts. The French physician Jean Astruc dis-

[5] See Conrad Wright, *The Beginnings of Unitarianism in America* (Boston: Starr King Press, 1955).

[6] See Robert H. Pfeiffer, *Introduction to the Old Testament* (New York: Harper, 1948), p. 46.

covered two sources within the Book of Genesis, distinguishable by the use of God or Jehovah as the divine name. The German philosopher J. G. von Herder (*Von Geiste der Ebräischen Poesie,* 1782) and the Anglican bishop Robert Lowth (*De Sacra Poesi Hebraeorum,* 1753) drew attention to the Bible as the literary creation of a religious people. Finally, as a premonition of things to come, the German professor J. S. Semler argued persuasively for biblical study free from theological preconception in his *Abhandlung von freier Untersuchung des Kanons.*[7]

Biblical scholarship flourished in nineteeth-century Germany. There the interpretation of the Bible had been partially transferred from the direct control of the churches to the rising German universities. German university scholars had recovered a view of the Bible's organic unity apart from theological systems, and, viewing the volume within the context of its own historical and cultural provenance, subjected it to historical and grammatical disciplines. These techniques were proving fruitful in the area of classical studies, and the German scholarly community was determined to treat the Bible, at least on one level, as it would treat any other ancient document. Although their critics often confused them with the earlier deists, these scholars, unlike the former, were motivated by an interest in critical analysis rather than by scepticism.

During the first half of the nineteenth century a group of New England thinkers began to assimilate the critical study of the Bible. They hoped to transplant to the New World the disciplines being developed by German scholars. New England liberals, later largely identified as Unitarians, attempted to use the new biblical studies as a destructive weapon against orthodox Calvinism. Convinced that traditional New England theology represented a distortion of the religion of Jesus and the Apostles, they attempted to restore primitive Christianity by means of a rational and scientific interpretation of scripture. Conservatives, sensing the real threat posed by the questioning of the theological authority of scripture, attempted to reestablish that authority by using biblical studies within the tradition of inherited Calvinism.

[7] Pfeiffer, *Introduction,* pp. 46–47.

At Harvard, which became the center of liberal biblical studies, the first academic appointment in biblical criticism was made in 1811. Edward Everett and George Bancroft received support from Harvard for their studies abroad with German biblical scholars, and by 1820 both had received doctorates from Göttingen. From Harvard Andrews Norton and George R. Noyes disseminated their rational interpretation of scripture and attempted to establish Unitarian biblical scholarship on a footing that would be both scientific and pious.

Andover Seminary became the center of conservative biblical studies. Moses Stuart carefully instructed his many students there, including Edward R. Robinson and Josiah Willard Gibbs, in the arts of biblical criticism, while defending the inspiration of the Bible and its final authority in all matters of religious faith and practice.

Biblical studies occupied many of New England's best minds, and theological battles between liberals and conservatives were waged over questions of biblical interpretation and scholarship. New works of German criticism such as D. F. Strauss's *Life of Jesus* aroused great interest in New England, and American thinkers demonstrated they were fully competent to assimilate and contribute to the already established tradition of biblical criticism.

Toward the middle of the nineteenth century, however, interest in biblical studies had begun to wane, in New England at least. Before the end of the Civil War the first generation of major American biblical scholars had died, and biblical studies ceased to play an important role in New England theological discussion. This seems to provide a natural limitation in time for the present study; the critical movement between 1800 and 1870 had its own rhythm of growth and decline, and when interest in biblical criticism revived in America it did not build upon the tradition established during these early years of controversy.

The reason for the geographical limitation of this study is not arbitrary, since it was only in New England that critical biblical studies made a considerable impact during the period. It is, moreover, limited to those men who demonstrated some real grasp of critical biblical studies or who entered directly into the general movement. The opinions of other prominent theologians and of the more traditional biblical commentators have been included only when required by the circumstances.

The history of New England biblical criticism is in itself a tradition worthy of the historian's attention. It stands out from other areas of American religious life that have previously interested historians, such as revivalism and the growth of social reform movements, by virtue of its scholarly and intellectual character.

CHAPTER I

A NEW WEAPON

Joseph Stevens Buckminster and the Beginnings of American Biblical Criticism

W<small>HEN</small> Samuel Dexter died in 1810 he left an endowment of $5000 to Harvard University for the promotion of "a critical knowledge of the Holy Scriptures." Until that time the study of the Bible had been the staple of New England divines, the butt of the deistic attack on Christianity, and the basis for the defense of the liberals against the traditional conservativism of their brethren. Within and without the churches discussion could be found in pamphlet, book, and sermon. Now, for the first time in America, the critical study of the Bible assumed its place in the academic community.

As a theological dilettante, Dexter typified the popular interest in the Bible in eighteenth-century New England. Although his father had been a clergyman and prepared his son for Harvard and the ministry, Dexter chose a more lucrative career in Boston commerce. He so quickly amassed a sizable fortune that he was able to retire at an early age and devote the remainder of his life to public affairs and theology. Belonging to the growing group of liberals who rejected the strict tenets of Calvinism, Dexter was concerned both to defend Christianity against the attacks of the deists and to preserve it from the theological distortions of the orthodox. Both goals could be accomplished, he thought, by "the increase of that most useful branch of learning, a critical knowledge of the Holy Scriptures." While others might merely urge the inclusion of biblical studies in the Harvard curriculum, Dexter possessed the funds to realize this ambition. His bequest inaugurated a new era in the religious life of New England.[1]

The President and Fellows of Harvard, with the special committee that administered the Dexter funds, soon established the first lectureship in biblical criticism.[2] In August, 1811, Joseph Stevens Buckminster was chosen as the first Dexter Lecturer.

Joseph Stevens Buckminster, son of a prominent clergyman of
Portsmouth, New Hampshire, was born in 1784. His father, a Yale
graduate and an orthodox Calvinist,[3] encouraged the development
of his precocious son, introducing him to the study of Latin grammar
and the Greek New Testament at the early age of four. The young
scholar distinguished himself at Harvard, where he excelled in the
classics and in rhetoric and added Hebrew and French to his fund of
languages. In recognition of his academic accomplishment he was
given a prominent role in the commencement exercises of the class
of 1800. After graduating at sixteen, he accepted an appointment at
Exeter Academy as an assistant instructor, joined his father's church
—upon public profession of conversion—and made known his intention to enter the ministry. Up to this time his religious opinions had
not strayed from the orthodox Calvinism of the senior Buckminster.

During the two years Buckminster taught at Exeter he began
reading for his chosen career. Had his father planned the course it
would undoubtedly have included Calvin and Edwards, but the son's

[1] A brief sketch of Dexter's life is included in Josiah Quincy, *The History
of Harvard University* (Boston: Crosby, Nichols, Lee, & Co., 1860), II, 296-98;
some of the will is quoted in the article "Dexter Fund at Harvard University,"
General Repository and Review, I (1812) 204-209.

[2] A special committee, consisting of five persons (three clergymen and two
laymen), was required by the terms of the bequest. The first committee con-
vened in May, 1811, and consisted of Samuel Dexter (the donor's son), Arte-
mas Ward, the Rev. John Bradford, the Rev. Dr. James Freeman, and the Rev.
William Ellery Channing.

[3] The term "orthodox Calvinist" is here used very generally. Of course,
there were a number of religious parties on the New England scene, but at the
beginning of the nineteenth century, the major parties were the liberals and
the traditional Calvinists. From the standpoint of the liberals all the right wing
parties were conservative. No attempt to distinguish these conservative parties
has been made in this chapter, because Buckminster made no such distinctions.
The terms "orthodox," "traditionalist," and "conservative," have been used in-
terchangeably.

journal mentions neither. His studies in Hebrew and in the writings of Josephus and his reading of Greek classics and patristics were traditional academic fare. Texts such as Grotius' *De Veritate* and Butler's *Analogy* were standard reading for young theologians, who needed the rational arguments developed by these Christian apologists to counter the attacks of deists and sceptics. But the peculiar theology of New England could be found in neither the Arminian Grotius nor the Anglican Butler. This early reading also included a careful study of Priestley's *Corruptions of Christianity* (1782), which argued that the original unitarian Christianity had been subsequently corrupted by Greek philosophy. At about the same time Buckminster also worked through John Locke's *Paraphrase and Notes on the Epistles of Paul* (1705–1707) in which Locke defended his thesis that the original Christian faith included only a simple belief in Jesus as Messiah. Locke argued that in the Epistles of the New Testament the original faith had been diluted by alien ideas and could be properly understood only when the positions of the several authors were carefully considered and compared with the uncorrupted preaching of the Gospels and Acts.

Buckminster continued to read English liberals and Unitarians when he left Exeter in 1802 to tutor his cousins in Waltham—a move which placed him nearer the Harvard library and his college friends. It is impossible to discover from his fragmentary journal exactly what he was reading, but it is evident that Unitarians, rationalists, and deists were driving him to more intensive biblical studies. A journal entry for 1804 reveals his growing concern. He was particularly upset by the arguments of Anthony Collins (*Discourse of the Grounds and Reasons for the Christian Religion,* 1724), who denied the existence of authentic Old Testament prophecies of Christ and at the same time implied that the New Testament references to fulfilled prophecies were falsifications. The English bishop Robert Lowth defended the authenticity of prophecy by a "two-level" theory, that is, that prophecies held one meaning for the prophet's contemporaries and another meaning for posterity. But neither this defense nor the argument of the German professor J. D. Michaelis, which was founded on the theory of accommodation of Scripture to the intellectually immature, was satisfactory to Buckminster.[4]

During this period other influences were pulling him from his father's orthodox position. James Freeman, minister of Boston's first avowedly Unitarian church, King's Chapel, was related to the elder Buckminster by marriage. Young Buckminster admired Freeman, and frequently worshiped in his church, and often visited his home in Newton. The combined influence of his reading and the circle of his acquaintances led Buckminster to question the theology he had inherited; he could find neither reasonable nor scriptural grounds for its support. His father was alarmed by indications of this change and placed the blame on Freeman. He urged his son to abandon the heretical influences of the metropolis and study with some orthodox minister in the country. None of the suggested ministers suited Buckminster, who was loath to leave the cultural climate of Boston. He carefully read every book his father suggested because he sincerely wished to please him, but he found all unconvincing. His life became a battleground on which the forces of filial love and parental authority struggled against the arguments of reason and the opinions of firm friends.[5]

The troubled youth wrote his father, despairing of ever "attaining . . . to those views which you deem essential." He confessed that his Christology was Arian (though not Socinian) and he clung to a firm belief that Christ had wrought man's salvation. But his integrity allowed him to accept neither the complete divinity of Christ nor the

[4] This problem continued to perplex him throughout his life. Isaiah 53 seemed so convincing a portrait of Jesus that he could not totally agree with Collins. But other prophecies appearing in the New Testament seemed to be forced. See Buckminster, *Sermons, With a Memoir of His Life and Character* [by S. C. Thacher], (Boston: John Eliot, 1814), p. 6; "Review of Sherman on the Trinity," *Monthly Anthology and Review*, III(1806), 254.

[5] A journal entry dated 22 December 1803 portrays this struggle: "O, that I could reconcile the commands of conscience, the claims of parental love, and the wishes of fond and partial friends!" Eliza Buckminster Lee, *Memoirs of Rev. Joseph Buckminster, D. D. and of His Son, Rev. Joseph Stevens Buckminster* (Boston: Ticknor, Reed, and Fields, 1851), p. 138. Pp. 131–55 describe the whole dimensions of the conflict.

satisfaction theory of the atonement. His father was so shocked that he bluntly answered, "you had better be a porter on the wharf than a minister with such views." [6] Caught between the alternative of surrendering his intellectual integrity to the demands of his orthodox father or entering the ministry with parental disapproval, Buckminster declined Freeman's offer of an assistant's position at King's Chapel,[7] and in the summer of 1804, his father consenting, he sought a position at Harvard as a tutor.

The Harvard appointment did not materialize and soon Buckminster faced another crisis. He had been asked to supply the pulpit for the Brattle Street Church, but his father objected: not only were his son's religious opinions heretical, but the Brattle Street congregation was too large and its membership too cultivated for a man only twenty years of age. The last argument was not without some weight: William Ellery Channing, Buckminster's senior, had declined to supply that pulpit because he thought it too demanding for a young minister.[8] At the request of his father, who thought that the Brattle Street Church would refuse to hear a man of such views, Buckminster frankly stated his theological position to the church officers. In a letter to his father he had expressed his conception of the ministry in this fashion:

> I have always considered it to be the object of the Christian dispensation to lead men to virtue and holiness, and that this also ought to be the great object of its ministers. To this end the doctrines of the Gospel are auxiliary as means or motives, without any intrinsic value in

[6] Eliza Buckminster Lee summarized her brother's position in this way: "He seems to have adopted the belief of the pre-existence of the Saviour, and of the connection of his life and death with the pardon of sin, while repentance and a holy life were also necessary." See Lee, *Memoirs,* pp. 149–52.

[7] Freeman's offer had depended on paternal approval. "[Buckminster] became in some degree involved in the design of Dr. Freeman to associate him with himself as a colleague, and finally to leave the labors of the Chapel pulpit to him. He had obtained a promise from him, that, with the consent of his father, he would . . . assist him in reading the Liturgy, and . . . preach in his desk." Lee, *Memoirs,* pp. 135–36.

[8] See James de Normandie, "The Manifesto Church," Massachusetts Historical Society, *Proceedings,* XLVII (1913–1914), 223.

themselves, or in the acknowledgement of them, except so far as they lead to this great end, the promotion of Christian excellence. If, then, I could believe that this great end could be attained without insisting upon Jesus Christ being the *most high God,* I felt no scruple on this score in endeavoring to bear a small share in this honorable employment.[9]

To the surprise of both, however, the invitation was repeated. Not without many misgivings, Buckminster finally agreed to supply the pulpit and shortly thereafter he was invited to accept a permanent appointment. Early in 1805, before his twenty-first birthday, Buckminster was ordained and installed; his father, acceding to his decision, preached the ordination sermon.

Because his father was so staunch a representative of New England Calvinism, Buckminster had become intimately concerned with the conflict between conservatives and liberals prior to his settlement in the Brattle Street Church. His own resolution of the conflict had been made on the authority of Scripture. In defending his liberalism on the basis of scriptural interpretation, Buckminster stood squarely in the tradition of earlier New England liberals. But his scholarly inclinations drove him to seek more sophisticated methods of biblical study than had previously been used in New England.

Buckminster's self-directed theological preparation placed him far in advance of his New England colleagues. He had already studied some of the best critical biblical works available to him. John Locke's *Paraphrase and Notes on the Epistles of Paul* had enjoyed a favorable reception in Germany; there his distinction between the nature of the Gospels and that of the Epistles made promising inroads into the traditional position, which regarded the Bible as a rigid unity, and which thus prevented the study of biblical writings in their particularity.[10] His study of the works of Bishop Lowth (1710–1787) was likewise of great value. Both Lowth's *De Sacra Poesi Hebraeorum Praelectiones*

[9] 23 July 1804, Lee, *Memoirs,* pp. 149–50.
[10] On Locke as a biblical student and his influence in Germany, see Werner Georg Kümmel, *Das Neue Testament: Geschichte der Erforschung Seiner Probleme* (München: Freiburg, 1958), pp. 55–59.

Academicae (1753) and his commentary on Isaiah (1778) had been translated into German. His work gave rise to a new understanding of the Psalms and the Prophets, for he was the first to point out the peculiar art of Hebrew poetic parallelism. Both J. G. Eichhorn and J. G. von Herder, Buckminster's contemporaries, built on the foundation he laid.[11] J. D. Michaelis' *Einleitung in den göttlichen Schriften des Neuen Bundes* (1750) had been translated into English by Herbert Marsh (1757–1839), Lady Margaret Professor at Cambridge, and Buckminster secured the translation. This important work was the first to treat separately the language, text, and formation of the individual New Testament books. Michaelis' *Introduction* daringly reopened the question of the New Testament canon, for he believed that only those books written by Apostles could be considered as inspired and canonical. Thus he forthrightly rejected Mark, Luke, and Acts from the canon, while raising serious questions about Hebrews, Revelation, James, Jude, and Matthew. Michaelis tempered this radical suggestion by pointing out that if the books were written by the authors whose names they bore, they could be accepted as reliable witnesses to history, and Christianity would lose nothing essential. He thus stayed within the bounds of orthodoxy, but he had raised some important historical questions concerning Scripture. Others who followed would not be so bound by traditional theology.[12]

With the appointment to the Brattle Street Church in 1804, Buckminster entered on a public career in which his biblical studies were to play a prominent role. In the ensuing public discussion between the liberals and the orthodox he would follow the same course he had pursued in his private struggles with his father.

In a Boston noted for pulpit orators, Joseph Buckminster soon was recognized as the foremost. He was referred to as " 'the seraph of the pulpit,' and never has there been in New England such rapt enthusiasm over a young preacher. He thrilled his hearers by an eloquence unique and unknown at that time—fervent, eloquent, glow-

---

[11] On the significance of Lowth, see Hans-Joachim Kraus, *Geschichte der historisch-kritischen Erforschung des Alten Testaments* (Neukirchen Kreis Moers: Buchhandlung des Erziehungsvereins, 1956), p. 108.

[12] On Michaelis, see Kümmel, *Das Neue Testament,* pp. 81–87.

ing." [13] John Thornton Kirkland, minister of the South Church and later president of Harvard, observed that Channing and Buckminster had revolutionized Boston preaching. Channing's preaching at the Federal Street Church was immensely popular, but contemporaries conceded that of the two Buckminster was the more powerful.[14]

Buckminster entered fully into the social and intellectual life of Boston. As one of the original founders and guiding spirits of the Anthology Club, a "society of gentlemen," he met for weekly dinners and conversation with the most distinguished men of Boston letters. The principal function of the club was the production of the *Monthly Anthology,* a journal devoted to the promotion of literature, the arts, and liberal religion, to which Buckminster frequently contributed.[15]

Buckminster's developing concern with biblical studies in the years between his installation at Brattle Street and his appointment as Dexter Lecturer at Harvard may be traced in the pages of the *Monthly Anthology* and in his published sermons.[16] Because of the prominence of his pulpit, his important position among Boston intellectuals, and the esteem with which the *Monthly Anthology* was regarded, his opinions were widely known and exercised considerable influence.

With the orthodox, Buckminster shared the firm conviction that

[13] De Normandie, "Manifesto Church," p. 230. This is no isolated tribute; it is repeated in different words countless times by Buckminster's contemporaries.

[14] In view of Channing's later fame, this is a surprising comparison, but one which was frequently made.

[15] See *The Journal of the Proceedings of the Society Which Conducts the Monthly Anthology & Boston Review,* M. A. DeWolfe Howe, ed. (Boston: Boston Athenaeum, 1910). Howe has given a list of the authors for the articles appearing in the *Monthly Anthology,* which were originally unsigned (pp. 315–29). The membership represented a kind of cultural elite. It included a number of eminent clergy—William Emerson, Joseph Tuckerman, John Thornton Kirkland, and J. S. J. Gardiner; several men identified with Harvard—Professors Joseph McKean and Sidney Willard, Dr. John Thacher; and men of letters —Arthur Maynard Walter and William Smith Shaw.

[16] The sermons were edited by George Ticknor, William Ellery Channing, and S. C. Thacher, who wrote the memoir to the first edition. The second collection was titled *Sermons, Now First Published from the Author's Manuscripts* (Boston: Carter and Hendee, 1829).

the Bible must be the final authority for all questions of Christian theology. To understand the Bible, however, required conscientious and scholarly study. While conservatives might *think* their positions were derived from the Bible, Buckminster was firmly convinced that, rather than using proper critical disciplines, they were in reality relying on creeds and dogmatic systems to interpret Scripture. As he wrote in the *Monthly Anthology*:

> The catalogue of American divines is not crowded with philogers [*sic*] and criticks, with scholars versed in the sacred idiom, and proved with the furniture of sacred science; but we discover in the villages and hamlets of New-England scholastic theologues, hair splitting metaphysicians, longbreathed controversialists, pamphleteers, and publishers of single sermons. . . .[17]

This unhappy neglect of biblical studies had obscured the purity and truth of New Testament Christianity. This very neglect was a primary cause of the dangerous rise of deism and scepticism. Buckminster told his congregation:

> If we would all first satisfy ourselves of the historical evidence of the gospel facts, and then each of himself carefully study the New Testament, and find his religion there, we should not see so many dogmatical, nor so many incredulous minds; we should not see the Calvinist passing into the Deist, the Atheist, the universal skeptic, and through mere want of repose, falling back into the bosom of an infallible church. No, it is from our having taken our religious opinions from authority, and not from the scriptures, that we see so much uncertainty and contradiction among Protestants.[18]

Buckminster's efforts in biblical studies were directed toward two ends: first, negatively, to show that the Bible, when properly understood, could not support the elaborate dogmatic schemes of the or-

---

[17] "Review of *A theoretick explanation of the science of sanctity, according to reason, scripture, common sense, and the analogy of things: containing an idea of God: of his creations, and kingdoms; of the holy scriptures: of the Christian trinity, and of the gospel system*, by Thomas Fessenden," *Monthly Anthology*, II (1805), 413.

[18] *Sermons* (1829), "Sources of Infidelity," pp. 145, 148.

thodox; and second, positively, to proclaim and establish true New Testament Christianity.[19] He employed two principal critical tools: a careful examination of the canon and inspiration of the Bible in terms of its history, and a study of the text of the Scriptures.

The Bible assumes a kind of rigid unity when God is considered to have so inspired the words of the received canon of Scripture that the human historical aspects of its composition and reception are of no importance. It is assumed that everything is written from God's point of view; therefore every sentence is usually binding on those who acknowledge the authority of God. While this position forces its adherents to harmonize every biblical contradiction, it does permit the Bible to be used as a simple textbook for doctrines. Passages may be detached from any portion of Scripture and synthesized into a dogmatic system apparently authenticated by the authority of God himself. This was the position of the New England orthodox as it appeared to Buckminster.

Buckminster contended that the Bible could not be used in this way. The whole historical process of the determination of the New Testament canon was shrouded in mystery, but from the writings of Eusebius he could demonstrate that several of the books now accepted as authoritative were of disputed authority as late as the fourth century. Following the lead of Michaelis, Buckminster concluded that the books of the New Testament were canonized, not because they were recognized as inspired, but because they were thought to have originated with the Apostles, who were inspired men. In writing the books now in the New Testament, these men communicated essential truths and facts that were binding on all Christians. But they also conveyed ideas and concepts that originated in historical context, and were peculiar to the writers and their audiences, and these ideas and concepts were by no means essential to Christian faith. In other words not all parts of Scripture were equally authoritative; the

[19] In the introductory memoir to the first edition of Buckminster's sermons Thacher wrote: "He was always of the opinion, that the principles of christianity, in their original purity and simplicity, were to be preserved, where they are lost or obscured, only by the study of the Bible, according to the maxims of a sound, and cautious, and enlightened criticism." Buckminster, *Sermons* (1814), p. xxxvii.

Bible was not itself the word of God but rather the vehicle of God's word.[20]

Buckminster developed this position in a sermon on the Book of Philemon preached to his Brattle Street congregation.

> By reflecting on the circumstance, that this letter is found in the canon of the New Testament, you may be led to form the most intelligible notion of what is called the inspiration of the book, and also to understand the most important use of the apostolical writings. You may thus ascertain, what it is that gives any ancient writing a place in your New Testament. You will find, that it is not because this writing or that was dictated by divine inspiration; for the question still returns, what proof is there, that this or that writing was inspired. But the true reason is simply, because we have sufficient evidence to believe it to be the work of an apostle.
>
> In an historical explication of the writings of the New Testament, such as we have now given of this short letter, would be found the most interesting and satisfactory mode of studying them. Instead of looking into every text, separated from its context, to find something which may bear upon a favourite system, we should be content to understand the apostles, as they meant to be understood by those to whom they wrote. We should learn, that they were not, on every occasion, delivering a system of dogmas for the instruction of all succeeding time; but that Paul, in particular, consulted the circumstances of his correspondents, reasoned with them sometimes on their own assumptions, and sometimes upon prevailing hypotheses, now according to their peculiar habits of interpretation, and then upon suppositions and accommodations of his own. . . .[21]

He explained to his congregation that the views of the gospel contained in the New Testament writings could be accepted as true, for

[20] "In order to understand the unconnected writings of any person, written at a remote period, and in a foreign language, the character of the writer, the opinions that prevailed in his time, his object in writing, and every circumstance peculiar to his situation, must be taken into consideration, before we can be sure of having reached the whole of his meaning." *Sermons* (1814), "2 Pet. iii. 15, 16," p. 167. See also, his "Abstract of Interesting Facts Relating to the New Testament," *Monthly Anthology*, V (1808), pp. 544–47, 580–85, 633–40.

[21] *Sermons* (1814), "Philemon," pp. 103–05.

God would not allow his chosen witnesses to falsify or obscure any essential aspect of the gospel.[22]

From his study of Michaelis Buckminster knew that some books of the New Testament might not have been compositions of the apostolic circle. Thus he distinguished between the "Received Canon" and the "True Canon." The received canon is simply the New Testament, that is, those writings accepted by most Christians as having apostolic authority. "The True Canon consists of those books only, the genuineness of which is established upon satisfactory evidence." [23] Defining this true canon was an unfinished task of biblical criticism. The specific evidence for each New Testament book must be examined, and each "sincere and diligent inquirer . . . [must judge] for himself what he is to receive as the rule of his faith and practice." [24]

But the greatest task of biblical criticism, as Buckminster saw it, was to separate the treasure of truth in the Bible from the earthen vessels that were its vehicle. As for Locke, the Gospels represented the principal locus of Christian revelation because they record the historical facts of Jesus of Nazareth, substantiate his life and message with fulfilled prophecy and miracles, and propound the one essential tenet of Christian faith: Jesus is the Messiah. Buckminster conceived of a kind of sacred history apprehended by faith in a manner not very different from the apprehension of secular history.

> By faith, we dwell upon those events, which are far beyond the reach of our sensible experience. In profane history we receive such facts with unhesitating confidence, and reason from them without suspicion. Why, then, should we not exercise the same confidence, when we contemplate events in the history of God's especial dealings, events, which have also the additional support of prophecy and miracle? By religious faith we are introduced into the counsels of omniscience, and see the hand of almighty power guiding, with unvaried wisdom, the wonderful vicissitudes of the world.[25]

[22] *Sermons* (1814), "Philemon," pp. 103–05.
[23] "Interesting Facts," p. 544.
[24] "Interesting Facts," p. 545.
[25] *Sermons* (1814), "Heb. xi. 1," p. 135.

Although the Old Testament was of secondary importance to Buckminster, he found its significance in this kind of history.[26] But the internal standard against which all Scripture must be measured was the history recorded in the Gospels: when any of the New Testament writings referred to these events, they were absolutely credible.

Buckminster entertained no doubts concerning the absolute reliability of the Gospels. They were substantiated by miracle, by fulfilled prophecy, and by their internal consistency. In a sermon on the character of Peter he contended that the consistent picture of this one figure found in the Gospels, the Acts, and the letters of Paul was in itself sufficient to establish the historical reliability of the New Testament.[27]

The internal standard furnished by the Scripture to discern the Word of God among the words of men could be supplemented by man's innate reason. In a remarkable sermon on the text of John 7:17, "If any man will do his will, he shall know of the doctrine, whether it be of God, or whether I speak of myself," Buckminster explained these criteria:

> The text gives to an honest and serious mind the liberty of judging of the claims, and even of the doctrines of Christ. That is, our Saviour does not profess to bear down the judgments of men as to the truth, either of his pretensions or of his doctrines, by the mere force of his authority. He evidently supposes some previous knowledge of God's will, some original truths, either of reason or of revelation, with which the professed communication from God must not be inconsistent. The

[26] Buckminster rarely dealt with the Old Testament. It did set the stage for the advent of Jesus; see *Sermons* (1814), "Fullness of Time," pp. 6, 7. Furthermore, the Old Testament relates how God dealt with men in the infancy of the race. "It contains the history of God and man in their connexion and intercommunication, and it is the only work which throws any satisfactory light on the origin, and progress, and destination of the human race, as moral creatures. We find there, it is true, many extraordinary relations, adapted to the infancy of mankind, and gradually becoming less frequent, as the faculties were unfolded and the moral notions of mankind were established. But even in the history of these, we find the same proofs of a wise providence, in the order and successive perfection of the different dispensations of religion, that we find in the natural growth and intellectual progress of individuals." *Sermons* (1829), "Providence of God," p. 130.
[27] *Sermons* (1814), "The Character of Peter," pp. 327–28.

text in fact implies, that in every case of revelation we have some stand-ard, more or less complete, by which we may judge . . . the doctrine delivered. . . . [Jesus] authorizes the exercise of reason in the case of revelation. . . .[28]

The criteria could serve to re-establish a pristine Christianity, and the critical understanding of the biblical canon and the inspiration of the Bible could demonstrate the folly of metaphysical theology.

Buckminster had been subject to frequent attacks of epilepsy since his days as an instructor at Phillips Academy; his health eventually declined so seriously that in 1806–1807 the Brattle Street Church sent him to Europe for diversion and rest. Although he made little con-tact with European religious leaders, he found theological works plentiful and cheap and expended a recent inheritance from his grandfather in gathering a library of 3000 volumes.[29] Perhaps the most important books he purchased were Griesbach's works on the text of the New Testament. In textual criticism, Buckminster was to discover a most powerful weapon to be used against the supporters of verbal inspiration.

Johann Jakob Griesbach (1745–1812) was a pioneer in German criticism of the Greek New Testament. His two-volume edition (1774–1775) of the New Testament was the first effective critique of the prevailing *textus receptus*. After a painstaking comparison of the manuscripts then available, Griesbach grouped the texts into three "families" and cautiously suggested some necessary changes in the prevailing text. The text was accompanied by a rich apparatus, and the work of Griesbach became the foundation for all later textual crit-icism. For the sake of convenience he issued an abbreviated "manual" edition of the New Testament in 1794.[30]

When he returned from Europe in 1807 Buckminster persuaded the officials of Harvard University to sponsor an American printing

[28] *Sermons* (1829), "John VII. 17," pp. 325–27.

[29] Buckminster's theological library was one of the best in New England. See *Catalogue of the Library of the Late Rev. J. S. Buckminster* (Boston: John Eliot, 1812). A microfilm copy is in Princeton University Library. The sale of the library after Buckminster's death was of great interest in New England. See below, pp. 27–28.

[30] On Griesbach, see Kümmel, *Das Neue Testament,* p. 88.

of Griesbach's manual edition of the New Testament. He had secured financial support from some of his friends, and his friend, William Wells, who was also a member of the Anthology Club, printed the work on his press. It appeared in 1809, and although Buckminster received no credit for its publication on the title page, he had carefully edited the proofs and corrected many errors in the German edition.[31] It was immediately adopted as a textbook at Harvard.

The publication of a critical text of the New Testament was an important event in the development of American biblical studies. No scholarly pursuit of biblical knowledge would have been possible without the basic tools such as texts, grammars, and lexicons. Although the publication of such books seems undramatic in retrospect, their continued appearance indicates the developing serious interest in scholarly biblical research.

In a series of reviews in the *Monthly Anthology*, Buckminster explained the significance of the textual criticism of the New Testament.[32] Obviously, any rational person aware of the history of the New Testament text could not hold to a rigid theory of verbal inspiration. Griesbach's careful collation of the many readings demonstrated that even employing the most careful scholarship, some contradictions could not be reconciled. It would have required a perpetual miracle to preserve an infallible text.[33] Furthermore, it could be historically demonstrated that certain inauthentic texts had been introduced; the most notorious of these was I John 5:7, a favorite proof text of Trinitarians. These erroneous texts had no more validity than the strange edition of the King James Bible that had given the seventh commandment as "Thou shalt commit adultery." [34] Buckminster noted somewhat sarcastically in a review of an American edition of the Septuagint that some might be surprised that Jesus and the

[31] Johann Jacob Griesbachii, *Novum Testamentum Graece* (Cantabrigiae Nov-Anglorum: "Published with sponsorship of the President and Fellows of Harvard University, 1809).

[32] Buckminster's articles for the *Monthly Anthology* were: "Notice of Griesbach's Edition of the New-Testament, Now Printing at Cambridge," V (1808), 18–21; "Review of Griesbach's New Testament," X (1811), 107–14, 403–21. See also his "On the Accuracy and Fidelity of Griesbach," *General Repository and Review,* I (1812), 89–101.

[33] See *Sermons* (1829), "Sources of Infidelity," p. 145.

[34] "Review of Griesbach," p. 110.

Apostles had not used the King James version.[35] He did not consider
Christian faith endangered by studying the Bible as one would study
any other historical text; for one thing, the results of textual criticism
had shown that the text of the Bible could be established more certainly than any other ancient writing.

Buckminster's knowledge of biblical studies was wholly derived
from English and German sources; he thought that this was inevitable since when judged by European standards the biblical sciences
in America were archaic. He felt it necessary that the American biblical student master European scholarship before he could hope to
make any contribution of his own. Buckminster himself was making
giant strides toward achieving this mastery; no anxieties about the
possible destructive effects of this criticism impeded his progress. As
he noted in his journal, "[I have] . . . the peculiar advantage . . .
of not being bound by a previous system of established dogma." [36]
He conceded that if essential doctrines and duties were threatened
by biblical criticism, then he would have to hold to fewer essential
doctrines.[37]

Buckminster did not hesitate to speak his convictions from the
pulpit, for he felt that the end result of biblical criticism would be a
purer and more defensible faith. He encouraged his friends to undertake the critical study of the Bible, and thus was directly responsible
for the great interest in this subject among many liberals. The young
Harvard scholar Thacher wrote:

> One of his strongest passions was, the desire to diffuse a love of bibli-
> cal studies; and the impulse among us, which has been lately given to
> inquiries on these subjects, is, in no slight degree, to be attributed to
> his exertions and example.[38]

Buckminster hoped to follow the publication of Griesbach's New Testament with the whole of his critical prolegomena, and to follow that

[35] "Review of Thompson's Septuagint," *Monthly Anthology*, VIII (1810),
194.
[36] Buckminster Papers, reel 1 (MSS, and a microfilm copy, in the Boston
Athenaeum Library).
[37] "Thompson's Septuagint," p. 194.
[38] Buckminster, *Sermons* (1814), pp. xxxvii, xxxviii. On his stimulation of
interest in biblical study, see also, George Ticknor, "Memoirs of the Buckminsters," *Christian Examiner*, XLVII (1849), 186.

with better texts of some of the Old Testament books.[39] He was particularly anxious that Harvard provide her students with a knowledge of biblical studies. In 1809 he gave the Phi Beta Kappa address at the university, and publicly encouraged the founding of a chair of biblical criticism.[40] There survives among his papers a petition apparently intended for circulation among Harvard alumni and designed to arouse enough interest among the wealthy to provide the necessary funds for the chair.[41]

It was no surprise, then, that in 1811 Buckminster was appointed first Dexter Lecturer on Biblical Criticism. He was the most qualified student of the Bible in New England, he was the most eminent of the Boston ministers, and he had urged the creation of just such a position. He immediately sent to Germany for new books and hired a German tutor so that he might master the works of Eichhorn and Semler.[42] He planned to begin his lectures in the fall of 1812, in accordance with the terms of the Dexter bequest. In June of that year, however, he suffered an attack of epilepsy, and in a few days, at the age of twenty-eight, the foremost student of the Bible in New England was dead.

[39] "In 1810 he formed the plan of publishing all the best modern versions of the prophetical books of the Old Testament. He proposed to use the version of Bishop Lowth for Isaiah, with the various renderings of Dodson and Stock in the margin, where they differ materially from Lowth. The major prophets were to be completed by Blaney's version of Jeremiah and Lamentations, Newcome's of Ezekiel, and Wintle's of Daniel, with Blaney's of the LXX weeks. Newcome's translation of the minor prophets was to have followed, with the most important variations from Horsley's Hosea, Benjoin's Jonah, and Blaney's Zechariah." Thacher, in Buckminster, *Sermons* (1814), p. xxxii.

[40] The address, entitled "On the Dangers and Duties of Men of Letters," is reprinted in *Sermons* (3d ed.; Boston: Wells and Lilly, 1821), pp. lxi–lxxxi.

[41] See Buckminster Papers, reel 1, "Memoir on the establishment of a Professorship of Sacred Literature." It may well be that Buckminster was responsible for the bequest in Dexter's will which established the lectureship in biblical criticism. Dexter's son was a member of the Brattle Street Church, and although no record of this direct influence survives, it is not an improbable conjecture.

[42] In May, 1810, Buckminster had written to Herbert Marsh, translator of Michaelis: "Such is the extent of my parish, & the variety of its duties, that I have neither time nor courage *at present* for the acquisition of the German language. And yet there are several points of theological inquiry which I burn to explore, & would willingly relinquish all knowledge of French for this single acquisition." Buckminster Papers, reel 1.

CHAPTER II

TRAINING THE GENERALS

Norton, Everett, and Bancroft: 1812–1819

W<small>ILLIAM</small> B<small>ENTLEY</small> could smell a bargain. For many years the bargain-hunting Salem minister had been building his own library of theological books; he fondly recalled how many of them had come from the auction of Charles Chauncy's library for only six cents each. In August, 1812, he sent a representative to buy a few books from the library of the late Joseph Stevens Buckminster, which was to be sold at public auction in Boston. His agent returned empty-handed.[1]

There were no bargains at the Buckminster auction. In part the high prices were due to the Napoleonic wars, which made the importation of European books almost impossible. But in large part the prices reflected the keen interest Buckminster's studies had aroused in Boston.[2]

---

[1] William Bentley (1759–1819) possessed a library of 4000 volumes, second in size in America only to the library of Thomas Jefferson. Although he was not an important leader of the group, he sympathized with the liberal Boston clergy. Through a book exchange with the German scholar of Americana, Christopher Daniel Ebeling, he collected a vast number of German theological and scholarly works. For a discussion of the Bentley-Ebeling relationship, see Henry A. Pochman, *German Culture in America* (Madison: University of Wisconsin Press, 1961), pp. 51–56. Bentley's discussion of the Buckminster sale is found in his diary entry for 30 August 1812: William Bentley, *Diary* (4 vols.; Salem: Essex Institute, 1905–1914), IV, 112.

[2] See *Catalogue of the Library of the Late Rev. J. S. Buckminster* (Boston: John Eliot, 1812). The copy in the possession of the Harvard University Library (microfilm copy in the Princeton University Library) contains manuscript notes of the sale price of some books and their purchasers. Andrews Norton described the sale briefly in the *General Repository and Review,* I (1812), 392–94.

The numbers of the *Allgemeine Bibliothek der Biblischen Litera-tur,* edited by the celebrated Eichhorn,[3] which Bentley especially coveted, were sold at prices beyond his reach.[4] Competitive bidding inflated the price of each number, which was originally twenty-five cents, to over two dollars.

The auction attracted a number of notable New England scholars. William Ellery Channing came because he had been appointed Buckminster's successor as Dexter Lecturer at Harvard and needed new books to prepare his course.[5] President Kirkland of Harvard came to buy books for the college library. Moses Stuart, recently appointed Professor of Sacred Literature at the Andover Seminary, came to buy books for himself and for the school's library. Edward Everett, Buckminster's young parishioner, who hoped to emulate his minister's erudition, came to buy books from the library of his mentor. These were only a few of the many scholars who gathered for two days, bidding until all 2300 of the offered books had been sold for more than $6000. Many years later, Moses Stuart recalled the excitement of those two days, highlighted by an intense competition between Everett and himself.

> I remember, with lively and pleasant emotion, the contest between him and me at the sale for Eichhorn's *Introduction to the Old Testament*; then a book unknown to our literary community. . . . We bid upon the volumes (there were four) until we rose above six dollars apiece, (for a moderate octavo on coarse hemp-paper); and finally I won the prize by bidding six dollars and a quarter for each volume. I have since purchased all four for as many dollars. Yet the acquisition of that book has spread its influence over my whole life.[6]

As he had wished, Buckminster's influence continued to be felt,

[3] J. G. Eichhorn (1752–1827), whom T. K. Cheyne called "the founder of Old Testament criticism," taught at Jena and at Göttingen. Influenced by both the enlightenment and the romantic movement, he was one of the first scholars to compare the Bible with other ancient writings.

[4] Bentley, *Diary,* IV, 112.

[5] Arthur W. Brown, *Always Young for Liberty* (Syracuse: Syracuse University Press, 1956), p. 457.

[6] Moses Stuart, "The Study of the German Language," *Christian Review,* VI (1841), 457.

and American theologians continued to turn their attention to continental biblical studies even after his death. He had written from Paris in 1807:

> Although I may, by the Providence of God, be cut off from the enjoyment of these luxuries of the mind, they will be a treasure to those who may succeed me, like the hoards of a miser scattered after his death. I feel that, by every book which I send out, I do something for my dear country, which the love of money seems to be depressing into unlettered barbarism.[7]

To a great extent, the development of biblical studies in America may be traced by following those who had come into Buckminster's sphere of influence, either personally or through the scattered treasures of his library. In the decade after his death, the movement may be followed in the lectureship in biblical criticism at Harvard, in the new conservative appropriation of biblical studies at Andover, and in the biblical studies of Americans in Germany.

Channing, as has been noted, was appointed in Buckminster's place as Dexter Lecturer at Harvard. However, he felt that these duties, in addition to those of his Federal Street ministry, were too much of a physical strain, and after one year (1812–1813) he resigned. Channing's concerns were not those of the critical scholar, for he felt that overintellectualism would endanger true religious feeling. He felt he could more adequately replace Buckminster as the leading preacher of liberal ideas. In Buckminster and Channing Harvard had lost the two foremost spokesmen for the liberal cause. The college next turned to the relatively unknown Andrews Norton.[8]

Norton, born in 1786, belonged to the same generation that had produced Buckminster and Channing. His father was a prominent

[7] Eliza Buckminster Lee, *Memoirs of Rev. Joseph Buckminster, D.D. and of His Son, Rev. Joseph Stevens Buckminster* (Boston: Ticknor, Reed, and Fields, 1851), p. 265.

[8] The only extended biographical treatment of Norton is by Allen S. Clark, "Andrews Norton: A Conservative Unitarian" (Honors thesis, Harvard University, 1942). Additional information may be gleaned from the Norton Papers (MSS in the Houghton Library, Harvard University), a collection not consulted by Clark.

lay leader in the Hingham Church, a church whose liberal minister, Henry Ware, was appointed, amid much controversy, to Harvard's Hollis Chair of Divinity in 1805. Norton, already sympathetic with the religious liberals, came to Harvard in 1801 and distinguished himself by graduating Phi Beta Kappa in the class of 1804. After a brief period of teaching in Hingham's Derby Academy, he determined to enter the ministry, returned to Harvard to read theology with Henry Ware, and received the A.M. degree in 1809.

During his second residence in Cambridge Norton was drawn into the circle of the Boston liberal clergy. Elected as an associate member of the Anthology Society, he contributed articles of literary criticism and several pieces of poetry to the *Monthly Anthology*. Buckminster frequently invited him to preach at the Brattle Street Church, and Norton's admiration for the eloquent young minister increased with this association. Even though Norton preached frequently in the pulpits of Boston's liberal churches, he was not offered an appointment. In 1810 he went to Bowdoin College as a tutor; a year later, however, he returned to Cambridge as tutor in mathematics.

During this residence, Norton was offered the position of editor-in-chief of the *Monthly Anthology*. Norton accepted, providing that he could be adequately compensated for his services and providing that the leading liberals would support and contribute to the publication under his editorship. He particularly desired to know Buckminster's feelings. But before these negotiations had been completed the *Anthology* had collapsed. Norton was selected as editor for *The General Repository and Review,* a new publication that drew its support largely from former Anthology Society members.

The editorial tone of *The General Repository* was markedly different from that of the *Monthly Anthology*. The *Anthology* had striven to be broad and non-sectarian; *The General Repository* boldly defended the principles of liberal religion against the orthodox. The mild Channing resented the militant sectarianism of *The General Repository,* and though eventually he too would be forced to defend liberal Christianity, he never forgave Norton's militant divisiveness and, years later, opposed his elevation to a Harvard professorship on these grounds.[9]

Despite the financial support of prominent liberal laymen and the contributions of Harvard professors and graduates, *The General Repository* could not find an audience large enough to justify its existence; publication ceased within two years. According to Norton, "It was too bold for the proper prudence, or the worldly caution, or for the actual convictions of a large portion of the liberal party."[10]

In the opening editorial of the first issue of *The General Repository*, Norton found occasion to urge the new principles of scriptural interpretation against the orthodox. In the strongest public attack heretofore made on the orthodox, Norton wrote:

> The modes of interpretation which [liberal and orthodox] Christians apply to the scriptures, . . . form characteristic differences. The orthodox [believe] . . . the writings of the evangelists and apostles to have been composed under God's immediate and miraculous superintendence . . . for the purpose of their being used and easily understood by all Christians in all countries and in all ages. . . . [They] apply to [Scripture] . . . a mode of interpretation very different from what is applied to any other book. They believe that no allowance is to be made for the inadvertence of the writer, and none for the exaggeration produced by strong feelings. They pay but little attention to that use of language, which is common in all human compositions. . . . They do not expect to find the meaning much disguised by peculiarities of expression of the writer or of the age or country to which he belonged; they pay but little regard to the circumstances in which he wrote, or to those of the persons, whom he addressed. . . .[11]

To this naive mode of scriptural interpretation Norton compared

[9] For a discussion of Channing's attitude toward Norton, see John White Chadwick, *William Ellery Channing* (Boston: Houghton and Mifflin, 1903), p. 154.

[10] Quoted by Brown, *Always Young for Liberty*, pp. 114–15.

[11] "Defence of Liberal Christianity," *The General Repository and Review*, I (1812), 2.

the liberal mode as developed by Buckminster along lines originally outlined by John Locke. The liberals considered all the historical circumstances of the scriptural writings, interpreted the Scripture as they would any other ancient writing, and regarded the preaching of the four Gospels and Acts as having authority superior to that of the other books. It was implicitly assumed that the Scriptures were to be viewed not as themselves inspired, but as the production of inspired men, and that the modern interpreter was to use his God-given reason to recover the meaning of the text. In this way the Scriptures could be freed from the foreign creedalism that had distorted their true meaning, and pristine Christianity could be restored.[12]

Although Norton's defense of the liberal position on Scripture was more polemical than anything Buckminster had ever written, it was, in fact, a summary of Buckminster's position. But whereas Buckminster had realized that this position might have to be modified, especially in the light of German critical studies, the editor of *The General Repository* clearly indicated that he regarded this position as normative for all liberal Christians, and that German critical studies were to be evaluated by its standards. In an editorial footnote to the translation of Eichhorn's "Biography of J. S. Semler," which appeared in the first number of *The General Repository,* Norton cautioned that, while the article contained much that was "valuable and interesting, there are some remarks in the free manner of the modern German school of theology which, for ourselves, we neither defend nor approve." [13] In a later number of *The General Repository,* Norton published Michaelis' refutation of Semler's interpretation of the scriptural canon.

In 1813 Norton received two appointments from Harvard College, one as Dexter Lecturer, the other as College Librarian. The first series of six lectures, which Norton delivered in 1815, were all directed to delineate the "character and condition of the Jewish

---

[12] "Defence of Liberal Christianity," pp. 2–3, 16, 25.

[13] Vol. I (1812), 58. Sidney Willard, Hancock Professor of Hebrew at Harvard, translated the article, thought to have been written by Eichhorn.

people" during the time of Jesus.[14] It is evident that Norton's critical study of the Bible was not far advanced; he shows in these lectures no awareness of critical problems nor of contemporary scholarship. Indeed they were so general in content that he later adapted them for sermons. But the officers of the college were pleased and asked that the next series of lectures be extended to twelve. By 1818 Norton was taking his duties as Dexter Lecturer more seriously and began to read Eichhorn's *Introduction to the New Testament* and the German periodical literature. In that year he also began a work on the "genuineness of the gospels," a work that would occupy his interest for the rest of his life.[15]

Although Harvard College officials apparently appreciated Norton's work as librarian and scholar, they did not consider him to be a specialist in biblical criticism. In 1818 he was offered the Professorship of Rhetoric. Even then a Harvard professorship was a coveted appointment, and it is surprising that Norton risked this position by appealing to President Kirkland, colleagues on the faculty, and influential friends to secure a theological appointment instead.[16] To John Gorham Palfrey, who recently had been called to the Brattle Street Church, Norton wrote a long letter outlining the arguments he thought might wrest an appointment in theology from the College.[17] Norton recognized that some liberals, notably Channing,

[14] See Norton, *Internal Evidences of the Genuineness of the Gospels* (Boston: Little, Brown, 1855), p. 296. One of the original Dexter lectures is included in the appendix.

[15] A manuscript of a journal of studies is included in the Norton Papers. In it he records his unfavorable reactions to his first readings of the German critics.

[16] Norton described this episode in a letter to George Bancroft, 11 September 1818. Norton confided that he thought he had little chance of procuring a theological appointment. The Norton correspondence is with the Norton Papers.

[17] Norton to Bancroft, 11 September 1818: "I wrote a long letter to Mr. Palfrey that he might show it to Mr. Channing, and to any other gentlemen whom he pleased. In this I stated my own conviction, that I should be much more useful to the University, and to the public as a theological instructor, and endeavoured to obviate the objections wh[ich] might be made to me as having been too open and decided on the expression of unpopular opinions; not by extenuating, but by stating fairly and justifying the course of conduct I had persued."

might object that he had been "too open and decided in the expression of unpopular opinions." But, he countered, he had only defended doctrines of "great *practical importance*," doctrines which he held in common with the majority of liberal Christians. Furthermore, these doctrinal differences must be aired because they involved the orthodox

> theory and rules of interpretation, . . . [the] notions entertained by them [liberal Christians] respecting the character and design of the Books of Scripture, . . . [their] metaphysical opinions . . . , their views of the nature, condition and duties of man, . . . their manner of regarding the facts stated in ecclesiastical history, and . . . their notions respecting the use of reason in matters of religion.

Norton suggested that most liberals could not be sufficiently trained to defend their own position in these crucial matters and must turn to some authoritative teacher. With notable lack of humility, Norton explained to Palfrey that he should be given a position of academic and religious leadership because "for a considerable number of years, the science of theology has been my principle [sic] study; and there is much both in the acquisition and communication of knowledge concerning it, which I hoped to accomplish hereafter." [18]

Norton succeeded. President Kirkland found additional funds, and the Dexter Lectureship became the Dexter Professorship of Sacred Literature. The events were significant not only as a turning point in Norton's life but in the life of Harvard College as well, for the theological department would soon become a divinity school. The subsequent history of the Harvard Divinity School and of Professor Andrews Norton played an important role in the history of biblical criticism in New England.[19]

Before Norton had delivered his first series of lectures, Harvard had made another appointment relating to biblical criticism. When in 1815 Edward Everett was inaugurated as Professor of Greek, the

[18] The quotations are taken from Norton's letter to Palfrey, September 1818.

[19] See Conrad Wright, "The Early Period (1811–1840)," in *The Harvard Divinity School*, George Huntston Williams, ed. (Boston: Beacon, 1954), pp. 21–78.

critical interpretation of the New Testament was included in his duties.[20] Norton thought that Everett's appointment "did not give general satisfaction," but that was undoubtedly because he had coveted the appointment for himself. William Bentley thought Everett eminently qualified for the position, and his appreciation of Everett's abilities was evidently shared by most.[21]

Edward Everett was born in 1794 in Dorchester. His father, Oliver Everett, had been forced into early retirement by ill health after a brief but promising career as minister of Boston's New South Church. The senior Everett had already identified himself with the liberal wing of the Congregational clergy and had been a close friend of James Freeman of King's Chapel. But he was to have little influence over the career of his son, for he died in 1802, when Edward was only eight. The family soon returned to Boston to live with the maternal grandparents. In 1807, at the age of thirteen, Everett entered Harvard, where both his brother and his father had gone before him. He distinguished himself in the entire academic curriculum and graduated at the head of the class of 1811.[22]

President Kirkland, who had succeeded Oliver Everett as minister at New South Church, had particularly favored the young undergraduate and when Everett received his degree Kirkland urged him to enter the ministry. As further inducement, Kirkland invited him to live in the President's house and secured for him an appointment as tutor of Latin. To Kirkland's urging was added the encouragement of Buckminster. The Everett family had become parishioners of the Brattle Street Church during their residence in Boston, and Buckminster had taken special interest in the gifted young student. Everett became a frequent guest at the Brattle Street

[20] Paul Revere Frothingham, *Edward Everett* (Boston: Houghton Mifflin, 1925), p. 35.

[21] See Norton's letter to his father, Samuel Norton, 29 February 1815, and Bentley, *Diary*, IV, 317–18, entry for 26 February 1815.

[22] Frothingham's biography of Everett may be supplemented by referring to Everett's "Autobiography," in his own hand (dated 1855), covering events until 1814, and Everett's "Autobiographical Sketch of Hon. Edward Everett," written in another hand and covering the period prior to 1819. (Both MSS are in the Library of the Massachusetts Historical Society; microfilm copies in Princeton University Library.)

parsonage and Buckminster soon aroused his interest in biblical studies and the liberal ministry, encouraging him to complete his theological preparation in Germany. Everett could not refuse such flattering encouragement.

In 1813, shortly after Everett had completed his theological training, the Brattle Street Church invited him to supply the pulpit, vacant since Buckminster's death; in November of that year he received an invitation to settle as the minister at that church, one of Boston's largest and most prominent. Everett accepted and assumed his duties immediately, being persuaded that he could not fairly insist that he first be given opportunity to complete his studies in Europe as Buckminster had advised.

Occupied though he was with the demanding responsibilities of his charge, Everett continued his critical study of the Bible. Stuart had outbid him for Eichhorn's *Introduction to the Old Testament,* but Everett soon managed to borrow the work, one volume at a time, and before leaving Cambridge commenced the laborious task of translating Eichhorn's German.[23] Soon he was projecting a publication of the entire work, although Stuart had advised him "to reject . . . those speculations . . . which would be obnoxious" to the American audience.[24]

Everett's work on Eichhorn was interrupted by a more urgent task. In 1813 a book appeared in Boston entitled *The Grounds of Christianity Examined.* In it the author, George Bethune English, an ex-clergyman, renewed the deistic attack on Christianity by questioning the credibility of the Bible. Even before Everett settled

[23] The Stuart-Everett relationship may be traced in eleven letters sent by Stuart to Everett, beginning 12 August 1812 and ending 14 January 1815. That the friendship could be so cordial between representatives of opposing parties suggests that lines of division in New England church life had not yet become so critical. Later both men largely ignored their early friendship. Nothing is said of Stuart in either of Everett's autobiographical fragments, and the reference to the spirited bidding at the Buckminster auction is Stuart's only reference to Everett by name. The letters are included with the Everett Papers (MSS in the Library of the Massachusetts Historical Society; microfilm copy in the Princeton University Library).

[24] See Stuart to Everett, 25 December 1813. In a subsequent letter (2 April 1814) Stuart indicated his only misgiving about translating all of Eichhorn was that it might adversely affect the book's sale.

at Brattle Street he had begun a book in refutation of English. Everett published his *Defence of Christianity against the Work of George B. English* in 1814, after the original furor over English's attack had subsided.[25] English was no match for Everett, who carefully refuted the new deist chapter by chapter, showing that English had based his work on bits and pieces of familiar deistic and Jewish writings without acknowledging his sources and that his plagiarism had resulted in gross inconsistencies. The Christianity Everett defended was that of the liberal party: the marvelous history of the Gospels was authenticated by the miracles and the resurrection of Jesus; the truth of the religion which Jesus taught was established by the successful dissemination of his religion throughout the corrupt classical world.

English's most cutting argument against Christianity he had borrowed from the English deist, Anthony Collins. English argued that the Gospel writers had pictured Jesus as fulfilling certain Old Testament prophecies which were not prophecies at all; in their abuse of the Old Testament, the Gospel writers had forfeited all claim to credibility. This was a particularly embarrassing question to those who pursued biblical studies along Lockean lines, for they felt free to criticize the Bible only because they believed that the Gospels afforded an absolutely reliable authority by which to judge all other Scripture. Michaelis had originated the standard defense with his theory of accommodation, which maintained that Jesus and the Gospel writers recognized that they were misusing Old Testament prophecies, but did so in order to appeal to an ignorant Jewish audience. In his *Defence* Everett daringly departed from this tradition, suggesting that the Apostles quoted the Old Testament "in a reference other than their original and true one" not to accommodate to Jewish usage, but because they were Jews and used the Old Testament in the same way that the rabbis employed Scripture in the Mishna. "It would be absurd to think that they would depart from prevalent style." [26] Everett's innovation turned the light

[25] Boston: Cummings and Hilliard, 1814. For background, see Frothingham, *Everett*, pp. 28–30.
[26] *Defence,* p. 240.

of historical criticism on the Gospels, a giant stride forward in biblical studies and a significant American development since it preceded a similar step by continental scholars.

The *Defence of Christianity* gave notice that the gifted young preacher who had succeeded Buckminster in the pulpit had also assumed Buckminster's position as the leading American biblical scholar. Like Buckminster, he was soon invited to share his knowledge at Harvard College, and after fourteen months as minister of the Brattle Street Church, he resigned to assume the newly established chair of Greek. That Harvard agreed to subsidize Everett's study in Germany made the offer even more attractive.[27]

Everett's scholarly sojourn in Germany was among the first of many; by 1920 nearly nine thousand American students had furthered their education in German universities.[28] Nineteenth-century German scholarship in the universities had been freed from church control. Indebted to Immanuel Kant's philosophical distinction between the real and phenomenal worlds, German scholars in many fields were dedicated to understanding the real world through rigorous logical analysis of observed phenomena. Classical scholars and linguists had at the same time developed systematic methods of comparative philology and saw the analysis of language as a key to understanding historical cultures and literatures. The convergence of these trends in the nineteenth century gave rise to critical textual analysis and a kind of historical criticism which demanded careful attention to the intention of a literature. This scholarship was immediately focused on the Bible and later gave rise to critical historiography and to historical schools in economics and politics.[29]

When Everett sailed for Europe in 1815, New England liberals were already anticipating the contribution he would make after he

[27] Frothingham, *Everett,* pp. 34, 35.

[28] See Jurgen Herbst, *The German Historical School in American Scholarship* (Ithaca: Cornell University Press, 1965).

[29] See Herbst, *German Historical School,* pp. 54–55. Herbst also gives a good account of the general interest in German scholarship among Everett's contemporaries, such as George Ticknor, Frederic Henry Hedge, and Joseph G. Cogswell. See also Orie W. Long, *Literary Pioneers* (Cambridge: Harvard University Press, 1935).

had been thoroughly drilled in a German university.[30] When he commenced his studies at Göttingen Everett abandoned himself to diligent study, allowing only six hours each day for sleep. Within two years he became the first American to earn a German doctorate. He spent three years travelling through Europe and returned to Boston in 1820. But the expectations of the liberals were to be disappointed, for Everett taught only classical Greek at Harvard. During his brief tenure there he made a lasting impression on many undergraduates, including Ralph Waldo Emerson, who admired his rhetoric as well as his knowledge of Greek literature.[31] But he made no further contribution to American biblical studies, and by 1825 he had left Harvard altogether to undertake a political career.[32]

Correspondence with his brother reveals Everett's vacillation both before and during his career as a student in Germany. While he expresses relief in leaving the Brattle Street Church—"such a degree of liberality as would have fixed me at B.S. [Brattle Street Church] would have been, I am well persuaded, fatal to my character, happiness and probably life"—he seems unenthusiastic about his appointment at Harvard—"I do not feel . . . to have got into just my place, though I confess I do not see any other likely to be accessible."[33] His theological and biblical ideas were marked by similar indecision. He began immediately to study with Eichhorn, Göttingen's most distinguished biblical scholar, but he explained that the study of Hebrew was not of great consequence to him and that Eichhorn himself was no longer the important scholar he once

[30] Bentley wrote in his diary: "[Mr. Everett] is appointed Professor of Greek language at Cambridge. . . . He stands among our first in New England. He tells me he intends a tour of Europe immediately. . . . We have never sent a man of greater learning since Norton [?]." "His establishment is to connect Greek literature with Biblical Criticism." *Diary*, IV, 317–19, entries for 26 February 1815 and 12 March 1815.

[31] See Ralph L. Rusk, *The Life of Ralph Waldo Emerson* (New York: Scribner's, 1949), pp. 76–79.

[32] Frothingham, *Everett*, pp. 36–92.

[33] Everett to Alexander H. Everett, 5 January 1816. The Everett correspondence cited in this chapter is included with the Everett Papers (MSS in the Massachusetts Historical Society Library; portions on microfilm in the Princeton University Library).

had been.[34] Still, he could not easily dismiss his "first love," biblical criticism.[35] He submitted his book refuting English to the faculty and expressed disappointment in their cursory review of it.[36]

One letter written to his brother in 1816 yields some insight into the forces moving Everett.

> I do not know that I ought to regret the time, I have spent in studying divinity, because it has probably made me feel easy in scruples, which had I known no more of the subject than those who pursue another profession generally know, would have troubled me much. But I tremble to think how near I had come to giving credit to that poorest of all systematizing, systematic Theology, of which the very terms are loathsome to me. With all this, I feel a strong attachment to the act of preaching; and sometimes think something might be done, to separate the public worship of God and the public teaching of duty, from all connection with arbitrary facts, supposed to have happened in distant nations and ages. . . .[37]

It is evident that Everett considered his study of divinity a thing of the past; thenceforth he would "pursue another profession." But he did not doubt the validity of historical and critical interpretation of Scripture.[38] Since Everett's problem was to find a way to separate the "public worship of God and the public teaching of duty" from the "arbitrary facts" discovered by historical critical methods, he evidently could find no necessary connection between arbitrary facts and religious truth. This seems to have been Everett's formulation

[34] Everett to Alexander H. Everett, 2 October 1815; Everett to Rev. John Abbot, 21 August 1817

[35] Everett to R. Walsh, 28 December 1817.

[36] Undated entry in Journal, "Journey from Amsterdam to Göttingen and Life at Göttingen, July 30, 1815–March 20, 1816." Everett's Journal is with his Papers.

[37] Everett to Alexander H. Everett, 5 January 1816. Everett was always the diplomat, and made himself as amenable as possible to all his correspondents. Thus, he could sustain a cordial relationship with Moses Stuart, although a frank discussion of their religious notions would have revealed many major differences. Even after Everett determined to quit biblical studies, he remained most cordial to Eichhorn. None of his correspondence, except two letters to his brother, shows that he was undergoing a major change of attitude.

[38] See below, p. 41.

of a classic theological problem, succinctly stated by G. E. Lessing in the maxim: "Accidental historical truths can never become proofs for necessary truths of reason." [39] The disparity between historical facts and truths of reason Lessing called the "ugly ditch." Everett had been reading the appropriate sections of Lessing and may have encountered this problem elsewhere.[40] He had come to the chasm and could find no way to cross. Biblical criticism threatened to undermine his religious faith.

If the "ugly ditch" were uncrossable, as Everett thought, the liberal program initiated by Buckminster was doomed to frustration. The liberals of New England had hoped to use biblical criticism both destructively, as a means of purging religion of the distorted metaphysical theology of the Calvinists, and constructively, as a means of re-establishing the pure and reasonable Christianity of the Gospels. But if historical facts do not necessarily yield religious truths, or if revelation cannot be authenticated by history, biblical criticism can become a tool that destroys liberal piety as well as Calvinistic orthodoxy.

Unfortunately, Everett felt no intellectual responsibility to share the results of his study.

> If I am let alone, I shall trouble nobody's faith or peace, but if I am not, I will do what has never yet been done,—exhibit those views of the subject of Christianity, which the modern historical and critical enquiries fully establish, stripped of the palavar with which the Professors here avail themselves, to appease the public clamour, and also unincumbered with the scandals of the French Philosophers. A sort of work, against which I can imagine no defence, except the very suspicious one of denying the premises.[41]

Everett had made a private truce with New England theology and

---

[39] Quoted by Karl Barth in *Protestant Thought from Rousseau to Ritschl* (New York: Harper, 1959), p. 137.

[40] See Everett's Journal, 3 September 1815. Everett had dicussed the so-called "Wolfenbüttel Fragments" with Eichhorn. Eichhorn felt that the questions raised were by then dead issues. But for young Everett, who had been, at least until that time, convinced that miracles actually performed were historical proofs of revelation, these issues could not be lightly dismissed.

[41] Everett to Alexander H. Everett, 5 January 1816.

the cease-fire was never broken. But a penetrating and well-trained mind had been lost to the cause of biblical studies.

Before Everett left Europe he wrote President Kirkland of Harvard suggesting that someone be sent to follow him at Göttingen. Perhaps at this time he indicated that he had lost interest in biblical criticism. In any case, the Harvard Corporation provided George Bancroft with a scholarship of $1700 per year for three years' study in Germany.[42] Bancroft, son of the liberal Reverend Aaron Bancroft of Worcester, was another of Harvard's precocious young men. In 1813, at the age of thirteen, he commenced his college studies. At Harvard Everett tutored him in Latin, and soon President Kirkland and Andrews Norton were taking an active interest in his education. Everett advised Bancroft to work in the area of biblical studies, since Harvard lacked a scholar in that area, and apparently this was agreeable to President Kirkland.[43] In a letter of introduction written to Eichhorn, Kirkland explained:

> [His friends] wish him to attend especially to philology, the ancient languages and Oriental literature, that he may thus be qualified to pursue theological studies to the greatest benefit, to give instruction as any opening may occur and invite, and become an accomplished philologian and biblical critic, able to expound and defend the revelation of God.[44]

Bancroft put himself under the guidance of his three mentors, Kirkland, Norton, and Everett, for he clearly hoped for an appointment to the Harvard faculty. In turn, he assured each of them that his religious faith would not be shaken by any German critical studies.

> I should be very unwilling to give my friends any reasonable ground for fearing that I should lose my belief in, or respect for Christianity. I do not myself believe, that my reverence for a religion, which is allied with every early and pleasant association, which, as it regards its evidence, has already been the object of my study, and which is con-

[42] For a biographical study of Bancroft, see *The Life and Letters of George Bancroft*, M. A. DeWolfe Howe, ed. (2 vols.; New York: Scribner's, 1908).

[43] Everett to Bancroft, 14 October 1818.

[44] Howe, *Bancroft*, I, 33.

nected with all my hopes of happiness and usefulness and distinction, can be diminished by ridicule.[45]

To assure Kirkland that his religious piety was not endangered by German scholars, he described for him the nature of German theological education.

The theologians form a very peculiar body. They have no idea of the sublimity or sanctity of their science. 'Tis reduced to a mere matter of learning. I never heard anything like moral or religious feeling manifested in their theological lectures. They neither begin with God nor go on with him, and there is a great deal more religion in a few lines of Xenophon, than in a whole course of Eichhorn. Nay, the only classes, in which I have heard jests so vulgar and indecent, that they would have disgraced a jail-yard or a fishmarket, have been the theological ones. The bible is treated with very little respect, and the narratives are laughed at as an old wife's tale, fit to be believed in the nursery.[46]

Everett's reaction to German biblical criticism had been primarily intellectual, leading him to the "ugly ditch" that prevented the founding of religious truths on historical facts. Bancroft's reaction to the German scholars was emotional: he could see that biblical criticism did not establish true religion because the most eminent of biblical critics were irreligious. Bancroft's emotional protestations against German scholarship served to establish a fear of German theology in America.[47]

By the time Bancroft received the Göttingen degree of Doctor of Philosophy in 1820, he had taken enough courses in Near Eastern

[45] Howe, *Bancroft*, I, 42.
[46] Quoted in Long, *Literary Pioneers*, pp. 120–21.
[47] Pochman writes: "Bancroft alone could not have been responsible, but it is more than a mere coincidence that henceforth, for fifty years to come, the accusations launched by him against German scholars and theologians are identical with those so widely repeated in the American press afterwards." *German Culture in America*, pp. 73–74. Norton suspected that Bancroft might be guilty of some exaggeration, but he wrote to Bancroft, 29 December 1821: "If you should, as I most earnestly hope, return uninjured in your moral feelings and principles, your character will have stood a severe and dangerous experiment." Some of Norton's fear of the Germans may be due to Bancroft's descriptions.

languages and in the Old Testament to prepare him for a career in Old Testament scholarship and enough courses in classical Greek and in the New Testament to prepare him for a career in New Testament research. But by that time Norton had been appointed Dexter Professor of Sacred Literature at Harvard, and President Kirkland was advising Bancroft to prepare himself to establish an American high school along the lines suggested by German educational methods. It seemed that Bancroft's preparation would make little contribution at Harvard.

Bancroft spent two years in Europe after receiving his Göttingen degree, including one winter in Berlin, where he took courses with Hegel and Schleiermacher. He returned to Cambridge in 1822. While in Germany Bancroft had been very much the American; in his letters to his friends he had expressed very anti-European sentiments. But in Cambridge Bancroft displayed his European education with conspicuous pride. Norton lectured Bancroft in severe language, expressing his keen disappointment in Bancroft's affected manners and Germanized conversation. Norton suggested that until Bancroft could conform to proper American standards of behavior the two should avoid all social intercouse.[48] The unhappy Bancroft remained only a year at Harvard as a tutor in classics and then left to found an American high school on a German model. He made no contribution to New England biblical studies, and is primarily remembered for his ten-volume *History of the United States*.

In the period following Buckminster's death, Everett, Bancroft, and Norton continued the liberal tradition of biblical scholarship. Everett left the field to keep the peace. Bancroft was excluded from the officers' club for social reasons. Norton alone remained to command the liberal forces.

[48] Norton to Bancroft, 15 September 1822. Letter is with the Norton Papers (MSS in the Houghton Library, Harvard University).

CHAPTER III

DEFENSIVE ARMAMENTS

Moses Stuart at Andover Seminary: 1810–1819

DURING the second decade of the nineteenth century, while Norton, Everett, and Bancroft continued the liberal tradition of biblical studies, Moses Stuart began his life-long project of reconciling new methods of biblical research with traditional Calvinistic theology.[1] Stuart, born in Wilton, Connecticut, in 1780, was a Yale man, graduating at the head of the class of 1799. Trained for a legal career, he came under the evangelistic influence of President Timothy Dwight while tutoring at the college, and turned from law to the ministry after joining the college church in 1803. Dwight supervised Stuart's ministerial preparation, and in 1805 the Center Church of New Haven called the promising young divine as their minister.

Soon the New Haven pastor had formed a friendship with Jedidiah Morse, the fiery leader of Boston conservatives.[2] Like his Boston friend, Stuart feared the growing strength of the liberal party and agreed that its heresies should be exposed and refuted. To that end he promised to write and procure articles for the *Panoplist,* the militantly conservative organ that Morse edited. Morse welcomed Stuart as an ally in the orthodox cause, for he recognized the success of his ministry and the high esteem with which

---

[1] For biographical information on Stuart, see John H. Giltner, *Moses Stuart: 1780–1852* (Ph.D. Thesis, Yale, 1956); and William F. Albright, "Moses Stuart," *Dictionary of American Biography* (New York: Scribner's, 1928–1944), XVIII, 174–75.

[2] On Morse, see James King Morse, *Jedidiah Morse, a Champion of New England Orthodoxy* (New York: Columbia University Press, 1939).

President Dwight and Connecticut Calvinists regarded the young preacher.

Boston conservatives had suffered a crushing defeat in the very year Stuart assumed his pastorate. At Harvard the Hollis Chair of Divinity and the presidency had both been filled by acknowledged liberals. Conservative candidates had been defeated. But soon, through the efforts of Morse and his friends, the conservatives regrouped; traditional Calvinists and Hopkinsians united in establishing a new institution for the training of orthodox ministers at Andover.[3] And to insure that the new seminary would not follow the errant path of Harvard, the two parties had agreed upon a formal creed, which each professor was to sign every five years. Andover would be safe from heterodoxy.

To the liberals, seeking to reform New England theology, the creed of Andover Seminary seemed to prevent the scholarly recovery of New Testament Christianity. The dogmatism of a creed distorted the simple essential truths of Christianity revealed in the Gospels. S. C. Thacher's review of the creed for the *Monthly Anthology* represented the most stringent criticism of the orthodox ever to appear in that genteel journal.

> [Creeds] are founded on the assumption, that the essential doctrines of Christianity are not *distinctly* and *explicitly* expressed in the language of the volume which contains them. It is implied in the very nature of a creed, that it professes to lay down the sense of the words of Jesus and his Apostles, more clearly and unequivocally in *unscriptural* expressions, than is done in those employed by Jesus and the Apostles.[4]

While he praised the founding of an institution devoted to the training of ministers, Thacher contended that Andover's creedalism

[3] For the history of Andover Seminary, see Leonard Woods, *History of the Andover Theological Seminary* (Boston: Osgood, 1885). Daniel D. Williams, *The Andover Liberals* (New York: King's Crown Press, 1941), pp. 1–7, presents a brief and readable account of the founding of the Seminary.

[4] The stress of the central authority of the "words of Jesus and the Apostles" should be noted. This was the key to liberal biblical studies. S. C. Thacher, "Review of *The Constitution and Associate Statutes of the Theological Seminary in Andover*," *Monthly Anthology*, V (1808), 609.

would retard progress in critical and exegetical theology, the very areas in which American studies had been surpassed by Europeans.

Thacher's misgivings seemed completely justified, for the conservatives could point to no counterpart of Buckminster in their midst, no biblical scholar of eminence. The Chair of Sacred Literature at Andover was filled by Eliphalet Pearson, who, after having been frustrated in his efforts to gain the Harvard presidency, had resigned his chair as Hancock Professor of Hebrew at Harvard and joined Morse in the founding of Andover. After teaching one year, Pearson resigned, and the Andover trustees searched diligently for a replacement. Finally they turned to Moses Stuart. Because of his recognized abilities, Stuart had seemed a likely candidate for a theological professorship. But since his knowledge of Hebrew and Greek was rudimentary, and since he was totally unaware of the critical pursuits of European scholars, it seemed unlikely that he would be invited to fill the important Andover vancancy.[5] However, conservatives could find no better qualified candidate, so in 1810 Moses Stuart resigned his pastorate and commenced his long Andover career.

Stuart's training under Timothy Dwight and his years of pastoral experience obviously did not prepare him for his Andover teaching duties. The constitution of the Seminary stated that the Professor of Sacred Literature was expected to deliver

> . . . Lectures on the formation, preservation, and transmission of the Sacred Volume; on the languages, in which the Bible was originally written; on the Septuagint version of the Old Testament, and on the peculiarities of the language and style of the new Testament, resulting from this version and other causes on the history, character, use, and authority of the ancient versions and manuscripts of the old and new Testaments; on the canons of biblical criticism; on the authenticity of the several books of the sacred Code; on the apoc-

[5] "I came here with little more than a knowledge of the Hebrew alphabet, and the power of making out, after a poor fashion too, the bare translation of some chapters in Genesis, and a few Psalms, by aid of Parkhurst's Hebrew Lexicon, and without the vowel points. I had not, and never have had, the aid of any teacher in my biblical studies." "On the Study of the German Language," *Christian Review*, VI (1841), 448.

ryphal books of both Testaments; on modern translations of the Bible, more particularly on the history and character of our English version; and also critical Lectures on the various readings and difficult passages in the sacred writings.[6]

With the prodigious mental energy that was to characterize his whole career, Stuart set about repairing the disparity between the description of his duties and his qualifications. He first turned his attention to the biblical languages, particularly Hebrew. By 1813 he had mastered the language sufficiently to prepare a grammar for the use of his classes.[7] In 1821 he imported a font of Hebrew type and printed a grammar for general circulation.[8] The long bibliography of grammars of Hebrew and Greek testifies to Stuart's continuing interest in biblical philology.[9] He was soon justly recognized as America's most competent philologist and grammarian.[10] The publication of Stuart's grammars, like Buckminster's project with Griesbach's New Testament text, provided would-be American scholars with essential tools for the enterprise of critical biblical studies.

No one profited more from the sale of Buckminster's library than did Stuart. His purchase of Eichhorn's *Einleitung ins Alte Testament* introduced him to German biblical critics, and, because he taught himself German in order to read this and other works, the whole wealth of German studies became accessible to him.[11] Stuart

[6] Woods, *Andover*, p. 235.

[7] *A Hebrew Grammar without the Points; Designed as an Introduction to the Knowledge of the Inflections and Idiom of the Hebrew Tongue* (Andover, 1813).

[8] *A Hebrew Grammar with a Copious Syntax and Praxis* (Andover, 1821). On this edition, see Albright, "Moses Stuart," pp. 174–75. This grammar went through six editions, the last published in 1840 at both London and Andover. "[This work] was commended by Dr. Nicol, Regius Professor of Hebrew at Oxford, as the best Hebrew grammar extant. The fourth American edition was accordingly reprinted at Oxford in 1831 and used as a textbook by Dr. Nicol's successor, Dr. E. B. Pusey." Henry A. Pochman, *German Culture in America* (Madison: University of Wisconsin Press, 1961), p. 573 n. 571.

[9] For a complete list of Stuart's grammars, see the Bibliography.

[10] However, to call Stuart "the father of biblical learning in this country," as does Frank Hugh Foster in *A Genetic History of the New England Theology* (Chicago: University of Chicago Press, 1907), p. 289, is misleading.

[11] Stuart, "German Language," pp. 448–57. Stuart's memory about his learning German is faulty. He remarks, p. 449, "A friend in Boston, who had

developed an insatiable thirst for the new learning, recognizing its superiority to all previous scholarship. He avidly sought to beg, borrow, or buy any German book dealing with the Bible, and was impatient because he could not read fast enough to avail himself of the material immediately.

Stuart's interest in German biblical scholarship was not shared by his fellow conservatives, who feared that the inevitable consequence of German learning was liberal heresy.

> No sooner had I begun to speak of some of the vagaries of German criticism, than some of my best friends began to feel a degree of alarm. It was not long before this became a matter of serious concern to them. Defections from orthodoxy had already become so fashionable at this period, in our metropolis and in its neighborhood, that more still were to be feared; and specially might it be my lot, as they apprehended, to fall in with this current, because I was avowedly fond of reading German writers, whose Liberalism began then to be indistinctly bruited among us. I was young, somewhat ardent, and withal not distinguished for sectarian zeal. The freedom and seeming fearlessness with which I indulged myself in reading critics of the looser stamp, was, in the view of many, a just and strong ground of suspicion that all was not well with me. . . .[12]

Cut off from his suspicious conservative colleagues, Stuart found in young Edward Everett a friend who shared his interests. Stuart and Everett had become friends before they competed for Eichhorn's *Einleitung* at the Buckminster auction, but eleven letters written by

---

studied theology in Europe, and lived for a while in Holland, presented me with Seiler's *Hermeneutik* . . . and this opened to me the world of German sacred literature. I perceived that I had not yet even passed the threshold, after some three years' labour here. . . . I—before I obtained Seiler—did not know enough to believe that I yet knew nothing in sacred criticism." Stuart's friend was undoubtedly Everett. But he did not leave for Europe until 1815. Stuart bought the volumes of Eichhorn in 1812. He undoubtedly had begun learning German before 1812, but he expressed great difficulty about translating Eichhorn's *Einleitung*. In a letter to Everett, 16 March 1813, Stuart wrote: "I know nothing of any books in that language [German], by perusal, except Luther's Evangelists, & Eichhorn's *Einleitung*." Stuart-Everett correspondence is with the Everett Papers (MSS in the Massachusetts Historical Society Library).

[12] Stuart, "German Language," p. 451.

Stuart to Everett are the only surviving fragments of the relationship.[13] In their maturity neither wished to publicize an earlier congeniality with a proponent of the opposite religious party. Genuine scholarly respect and exchange of opinions such as the two young students sustained during the period 1812–1814 became increasingly rare in a New England divided by theological differences.

Stuart projected an ambitious program for the young Cambridge tutor, who did not have so demanding a teaching load as he. In the summer of 1812 Stuart invited Everett to his Andover home for an overnight visit. With pride he showed Everett the beginnings of his German library and urged him to borrow and translate some theological works of Herder.[14] In a few months he was offering to take the coveted volumes of Eichhorn from the Seminary library in his name and lend them to Everett a volume at a time so that the treasures of the German critic could be shared.[15] When Everett began to preach at Brattle Street, Stuart discouraged his taking a ministerial charge, arguing that such a course would curtail his studies.[16]

Stuart shared with Everett the joyous discovery of an immigrant German minister in New York who was willing to sell a few precious German volumes.[17] And Stuart confided some of his personal problems to his liberal friend. He could not find sufficient time to read and study and could only read the portions of Eichhorn that immediately applied to his Old Testament lectures.[18] William Bentley, who had such a fine library of German theology in Salem, would not lend his books to Stuart. Stuart wrote to Everett:

> I want you to go & pay a visit to *Bentley,* in Salem. The *Old democrat* won't lend me his books, because I belong to Andover Seminary:

[13] See above, p. 36 n. 23.

[14] Stuart to Everett, 12 August 1812. Stuart finally succeeded in getting Herder translated by his pupil James Marsh: Johann Gottfried von Herder, *The Spirit of Hebrew Poetry* (Burlington, Vermont: E. Smith, 1833).

[15] "With very great pleasure I will loan it to you, as I can take it out, on my own account, & can send it to you without any necessity of telling our Librarian that I mean to so dispose of it." Stuart to Everett, 13 February 1813.

[16] See Stuart to Everett, 24 June 1813.

[17] Stuart to Everett, 9 July 1813.

[18] Stuart to Everett, 16 March 1813.

at least, I suspect this is the case. He has a high opinion of you; & I do not doubt will lend you Plank, or Reinhard, or Eichhorn, or any thing else which he has.[19]

In his intellectual isolation Stuart longed for a select "oriental club"; he urged Everett to seek some Cambridge scholars for such a group and to invite Stuart to join.[19] Finally Stuart, reflecting his concern over criticism of his colleagues, confessed some misgivings about his situation at Andover: "I hope I am honest in my attachment to the Creed of this Seminary, but I am very far from opposing investigation and discussion." [20]

But Stuart and Everett did not always agree. Stuart, for all his admiration of Eichhorn, found that "[his] . . . theological sentiments . . . are very widely different from my own." [21] Everett sympathized more fully with the German scholar and planned to publish Eichhorn's entire *Einleitung* in translation, although Stuart objected that some parts were "obnoxious." [22]

In one of the last letters Stuart wrote to Everett he expressed his hopes that the new biblical studies would unite rather than separate the two New England religious parties.

I hope the day of bitterness & personal enmity in the great controversy now pending is passing away; & that both parties will feel more necessity of critical investigation, of understanding the *original,* of settling the laws of interpretation, & the degree of credit due to the Sacred writers. The ultimatum must rest wholly on this so far as fair dispute is con[cerned]. It being once settled that the decisions of Scriptures are b[indin]g *in all cases,* & that the Bible is to be interpreted as other books. . . . Fair minds, who love truth; & will investigate it, in view of the judgment seat of Christ, will be very apt to entertain at last the same opinions, on all essential matters.[20]

On this note of hope the Stuart-Everett correspondence abruptly ceases. Possibly Stuart read Everett's *Defence of Christianity* and realized that Everett's approach to the Bible threatened traditional the-

[19] Stuart to Everett, 14 January 1815.
[20] Stuart to Everett, 14 May 1814.
[21] Stuart to Everett, 13 February 1813.
[22] See above, p. 36.

ology. Cut off from his liberal friend and suspected by his fellow conservatives, Stuart was forced into scholarly isolation. When, five years later, Stuart again discussed the authority of Scripture with a representative of the liberal party, the discussion took the form of a pamphlet debate. Stuart and his liberal opponent, William Ellery Channing, had come to very different conclusions as the result of their biblical studies: the study of the Bible had divided rather than united New England Christians.

Stuart's suggestion to Everett that the Bible be "interpreted as other books" seems a daring concession for a conservative Calvinist. On the basis of such a hypothesis earnest biblical critics pursued a course which threatened theological traditions built on the basis of a pre-critical doctrine of scriptural authority. And in New England the liberal party had been seeking to exploit this critical threat in order to overthrow the hegemony of Calvinism.

Actually, as the notes for his early Andover lectures demonstrate, Stuart set strict limitations upon his willingness to study Scripture as simply another ancient book.[23] The Andover Creed, which he endorsed, stated that the Bible "contained the word of God" and represented "the only pefect rule of faith and practice." [24] Stuart carefully stood within this creed, although he stretched it as far as possible to make room for biblical criticism. He maintained that biblical language must be understood according to the linguistic tools applied to any literature.[25] He advocated a "grammatico-historical interpretation" of the Bible which would fully consider "everything belonging to [the] grammar, rhetoric, & history" of a particular biblical author and his audience.[26] Finally, he conceded to the critics that "on all subjects, not pertaining directly to the development of moral or religious truth . . . the sacred writers [express] the common views of their age & time." [26]

[23] Stuart's lecture notes on the Old Testament and Hermeneutics, both apparently dating from the early part of his career, are included in the Stuart Papers (MSS at the Andover-Newton Theological Library; a microfilm copy is in the Yale Divinity School Library). References to these lectures will be made by series and by the Roman numeral that indicates the particular lecture.

[24] Woods, *Andover,* p. 248.

[25] Hermeneutics, II.

[26] Hermeneutics, VI.

Stuart had to make these concessions to the biblical critics, for he was intellectually convinced of the validity of their research. But the difficulties involved in harmonizing traditional theology with new biblical science become apparent. It was inconsistent for one who maintained the absolutely binding authority of Scripture to concede that some extra-biblical standard could be employed to distinguish moral and religious truth from historical adiaphora. The liberal critics, after all, were merely defining moral and religious truth in their own terms and enlarging the area of the Bible that they chose to refer to as the historical context of Scripture. Logically, Stuart could not quarrel with the methods of this enterprise; he could only defend a different view of religious truth—a different theology.

The conception of religious truth under which Stuart operated included a view of Scripture as the inspired word of God. This doctrine made the Bible a book unlike any other and demanded a strict limitation upon the consideration of it as a reflection of its historical context. Stuart did not lecture on the inspiration of the Bible, for he felt the treatment of that subject lay within the department of Christian theology. He did tell his students that it was a doctrine that could be "satisfactorily proved to every candid and ingenious mind." [27] Further, Stuart offered to substantiate the doctrine of inspiration in his Old Testament lectures by proving the genuineness, the authenticity, and the canonicity of the Old Testament books.

Stuart understood canonicity and inspiration to be "substantially synonymous" terms.[28] He conceived that the Old Testament canon was closed shortly after the Jews returned from the Babylonian captivity and that in the time of Jesus the Jews regarded the Old Testament as the product of prophets and inspired writers. Jesus and the Apostles never attempted to contradict this point of view, and indeed referred to those books when they gave religious instruction to the Jews. Thus the authority of a canon substantiated by Jesus and the Apostles gave weight to the doctrine of inspiration, which could be further proved by the internal evidence of the actual "*matter* of t[he] composition." [29]

[27] Old Testament, VIII.
[28] Old Testament, XI.
[29] "By canonical books, I understand those books to wh[ich] Christ & his

In a way this was a well-conceived argument to urge against those who, following Locke, had supposed they could freely criticize the Old Testament on the basis of the rational religion found in the Gospels, for Stuart was showing that an acceptance of Old Testament authority could be established within the Gospels. But since, Michaelis, biblical critics had considered that Jesus and the Apostles had used the Old Testament merely to accommodate to Jewish prejudice. Edward Everett, going beyond this position, had maintained that the use of the Old Testament in the Gospels reflected the use of typical first-century Jewish exegesis among the earliest Christians. Stuart's argument for the canonicity and inspiration of the Old Testament was not without its logical difficulties. He admitted that the early church, which had created the canon, had not considered canonicity to have anything to do with authority or inspiration. The canon of Scripture had simply encompassed those books thought suitable for public worship. But Stuart thought this view could be readily dismissed since the church fathers were not good critics.[30] This left the question of the canonicity and inspiration of the New Testament unresolved, for if the early church did not understand the categories of canonicity properly, whence the authority of the New Testament? And if the question of the inspiration of the New Testament is unresolved, how can it be used to substantiate the Old?

To maintain the authority of the Old Testament Stuart thought it also necessary to demonstrate the genuineness and authenticity of the individual books. This in turn required a demonstration that "they were composed not by impostors, but by the men who have always been commonly reputed to be their authors, . . . about the

---

Apostles referred when they gave religious instruction to t[he] Jews as decisive in respect to all matters of wh[ich] th[ey] treat; & wh[ich] were regarded by the Jews of th[e] day, particularly t[he] Jews of Palestine, as being t[he] genuine books of their prophets & inspired writers." "In this sense, *canonical* and inspired are not perfectly synonymous." "[But they] are substantially synonymous." Old Testament, XI.

[30] "We wish to know what books t[he] Apostles, & Jews of their day regarded as Canonical; & having satisfactory evidence of this, we feel no obligation to be guided by t[he] individual opinion of this or that Chr[istian] Father." Old Testament, XIV.

time . . . they are said to have been written." [31] The authenticity of
the Old Testament writings concerned the demonstration that they
were "worthy of all credibility." This task belonged to the theological department, but it was important to Stuart, who assured his students that even an anonymous book or a book that had been im-
properly attributed to an author might still be authentic.[31]

So, conceiving it essential to prove the genuineness of the Old
Testament books, this nineteenth-century Moses set out to show that
3400 years earlier his namesake had written the Pentateuch. Biblical critics, who were finding different documents within the Pentateuch and denying the Mosaic authorship of the whole, supposed that
early scriptural writing had originated in the infancy of the human
race, when conventions of authorship were imprecise. Stuart lacked
the historical perspective of German critics. He did not subject the
Bible to thoroughgoing historical criticism, for he could not fully
accept the fact that human conventions and forms of thought change
from age to age. He supposed that men in ancient times were like
men in modern times and that the tradition of the Mosaic authorship of the Pentateuch would not have been accepted by rational Israelites unless it was a well-authenticated tradition. Supposing that
ancient compilers must have been like modern compilers, Stuart argued that no hypothetical editor of the Pentateuch would have included such material as the instruction for building the tabernacle;
these plans had value only for those who built it. Nor would an assumed compiler have inserted new laws that superseded previous
legislation.

> The Pent[ateuch] claims Moses as its author. It . . . has always
> been considered as one book, . . . the work of one man. . . . The
> parts of it, historical and perceptive stand in such connection that
> they cannot be separated. . . .[32]

Stuart was prepared to make some concessions to the critics. Some
place names had been added to the Pentateuch after Moses. It had
to be admitted that the critics had discovered a number of sources
within the book of Genesis.

[31] Old Testament, X.
[32] Old Testament, XV.

> Perhaps . . . Moses [did not compose] this book in the same man-
> ner, in all respects, as he did t[he] history of his own times. It is not
> necessary in either case, to suppose th[at] he was inspired in such a
> sense, as to supersede all inquiries on his part, or t[he] use of his
> senses & understanding. It is enough for t[he] credibility & authen-
> ticity of t[he] books, th[at] he was moved by t[he] Holy Spirit to
> write them; th[at] he was divinely illuminated as to things unattain-
> able by t[he] exercise of his mental powers; & th[at] as to historical
> facts, his narration was preserved, by the power th[at] aided him,
> free from all error.[33]

Stuart had attempted to solve a critical problem theologically. Since
multiple authorship of Genesis threatened the book's genuineness
and authenticity, and since he could not reasonably deny the existence of sources within the book or maintain that Moses could have
had direct access to them, he had turned to the dogma of inspiration
for a defense of its Mosaic authorship.

Similarly, in his lecture on Isaiah, Stuart defended the unity of
the book against the attack of Eichhorn. He maintained that events
described in the last portion of the book show that the prophet was
inspired, not that the writer was contemporary with the events. Eichhorn, Stuart felt, was guilty of bad theology, for he had assumed that
the book was *not* inspired.

> All t[he] objections drawn from t[he] *matter* of Isaiah's prophecies,
> against their genuineness, are quite inconclusive, when once t[he]
> inspiration of t[he] prophet is admitted. To assume th[at] he was
> not inspired, & then to [move on?] from this assumption against
> t[he] genuineness of t[he] works attributed to him, is not a fair
> mode of reasoning. Let it first be shewn, contrary to t[he] assertion
> of C[hrist] & his Apostle th[at] he was not inspired, & we shall be
> bound to give t[he] arguments wh[ich] have been examined a con-
> sideration.[34]

Again, Stuart solved a critical problem dogmatically.

The Book of Ecclesiastes presented a more acute problem. Stuart
could not conceive how Solomon could possibly have been the author

---

[33] Old Testament, VIII.
[34] Old Testament, XXXVII.

of the book, since the language and style differed so radically from that of Solomon's proverbs. While Stuart lacked the historical acumen to follow German criticism, he was capable of grammatical criticism. Since no doctrine of inspiration could explain a difference of style, he was forced to give his students a precis of critical comments on the book. He concluded the lecture by expressing the hope that some pious critic could soon resolve all difficulties.

> As you perceive, I have scarcely expressed any opinion of my own. The reason of this is, th[at] I have not been able to form one, wh[ich] sh[ould] satisfy my own mind, or the reasons of which w[ould] give satisfaction to you. . . . An introduction to this book, & a comment upon it, wh[ich] w[oul]d give satisfaction to t[he] pious & intelligent Chr[istian], who believes in t[he] divine authority of t[he] holy [Scriptures], are yet a desideratum in t[he] province of Sacred Literature. I wait with anxiety for t[he] time when these shall appear.[35]

Stuart supposed, surprisingly, that the last seven chapters of Jeremiah and the first six chapters of Ezra were not written by the men whose names they bore.[36] Following Eichhorn, he granted that the Book of Judges did not contain a chronological history of Israel, but attempted to demonstrate the consequences of national sin by historical example.[37] For some reason, Stuart's faith in the authority of the Bible was not threatened by these critical conclusions.

Throughout his critical studies Stuart assumed that the Bible was an absolute unity, because God had inspired the entire corpus of the writings. He could find no contradictions in the writings, but only a few discrepancies in names and numbers, which were attributable to the faulty transmission of text. The Bible contained a system of doctrine readily apprehendable by the intelligent scholar. Stuart could even use this theological conception as a critical tool, for he could resolve difficulties in one passage of Scripture by referring to a clear statement in another passage.

[35] Old Testament, XXXIV.
[36] Old Testament, XXVIII, XXXVIII.
[37] Old Testament, XXIV.

> When I am persuaded that the whole of the [Scriptures] are *one system* of revealed truth, I am at liberty to quote from the whole, in a certain sense as the works of one author, in order to illustrate what is obscure by what is plain.[38]

Quite out of keeping with this whole approach to the authority and nature of the Bible, Stuart also proposed a doctrine of progressive revelation.

> The earlier part of revelation is merely inceptive; not designed as a full and complete development of a perfect religion, but adapted to the earlier state of the world. More of sensible objects are presented in these early communications than in the later periods of revelation, when it was made in a manner more spiritual, & perfect.[39]

The notion of progressive revelation does not harmonize well with a doctrine of the absolute unity of the Bible, for if its form and content reflect human historical origins, how can it be regarded as one system of truth originating with God? From German critics Stuart had derived the concept of progressive revelation, a concept to which he was strongly attracted as a nineteenth-century rationalist. He had derived the doctrine of the absolute unity of the Bible from his orthodox Calvinism, and his whole orientation toward New England theology demanded that he maintain this view. He did not attempt to reconcile this contradiction; he was probably quite unaware of it.

By 1819 Moses Stuart had become thoroughly acquainted with recent biblical scholarship. He was probably the best-read scholar in the subject in New England, and his lectures at Andover represented a much broader understanding of biblical literature than those of Andrews Norton at Harvard. Stuart had appropriated for himself much of the methods and conclusions of the new science. But the basis of his orientation toward the Bible was dogmatic rather than scientific. His hope for reconciliation between the two religious parties on the basis of biblical knowledge was both baseless and short-lived: the dogmatic principles Stuart employed in his biblical re-

[38] Hermeneutics, III.
[39] Hermeneutics, II.

searches were precisely those principles that the liberals disputed. Stuart had accepted so much of the new learning that his own position could not be consistently synthesized. He was caught in the tension of being at the same time an evangelical Calvinist and a rationalistic American.

CHAPTER IV

CHARGE AND COUNTER-CHARGE

Channing's Baltimore Sermon

L IBERALS of the Boston area were delighted when the new liberal society in Baltimore looked to New England for leadership in 1819 by calling Jared Sparks, a Harvard graduate and a parishioner of Channing's Federal Street congregation, to be their minister. Unitarian societies had been founded by Joseph Priestley in Philadelphia before the turn of the century, but these were direct English transplants, and not at all like the native American species of the Northern States. The ordination of one of their own number in Baltimore was a propitious event, and New England liberal leaders responded by making the long trip to support the new minister and the new society. Their most effective preacher, William Ellery Channing, was fittingly invited to deliver the ordination sermon.[1]

Channing's sermon, entitled "Unitarian Christianity," has been called the "Pentecost of American Unitarianism." The simile is apt, for the sermon served as a unifying force among American religious liberals. In it Channing clearly delineated the tenets by which the liberals were distinguishable from their orthodox colleagues. The liberals circulated the sermon widely, and Channing's clear definition of American Unitarianism became the focal point of charge and counter-charge on the religious battlefield.[2]

---

[1] See John White Chadwick, *William Ellery Channing* (Boston: Houghton Mifflin, 1903), pp. 145, 148; and Arthur W. Brown, *Always Young for Liberty* (Syracuse: Syracuse University Press, 1956), pp. 124–37.

[2] Brown, *Always Young,* p. 131; Chadwick, *Channing,* p. 147. The printed sermon's circulation exceeded that of any American publication prior to the printing of the Webster-Hayne debate of 1830.

Channing had accepted the Unitarian label in 1815. American liberals had long sympathized with English Unitarians and had read their writings with interest and profit. Nevertheless, American liberals felt that their movement was peculiarly their own, and men like Channing and Buckminster could not accept the English Unitarians' portrayal of Jesus as a mere man.[3]

But Jedidiah Morse, the fiery editor of the *Panoplist*, had long desired to expose the heterodoxy of the liberals, to pin them with a definite label, and to quarantine them from the fellowship of orthodox churches. In 1815 he acquired a copy of Thomas Belsham's *Memoirs of the Life of the Rev. Theophilus Lindsey*, which had appeared in England in 1812. One chapter of Belsham's book concerned American Unitarianism; Morse prefaced this chapter with ten pages of his own, gave it the title *American Unitarianism*, and financed its publication as a separate work. In it Morse accused American liberals of dishonestly concealing their heterodoxy, identified them closely with English Unitarianism, and demanded that they therefore be excluded from the fellowship of the orthodox.[4]

Channing in rebuttal defended the liberals in his pamphlet *A Letter to the Rev. Samuel C. Thacher, on the Aspersions Contained in a Late Number of the Panoplist, on the Ministers of Boston and the Vicinity*.[5] Channing argued that the majority of New England liberals could not accept the Christology, the materialism, or the republicanism of English Unitarians. Hence, American liberals had concealed nothing. Channing denied that the question of the Trinity had central significance for his party: they only desired to maintain a simple scriptural Christianity. With these qualifications clearly understood, Channing was willing to accept the Unitarian label, for he was certain that no doctrine of the Trinity could be found in Scripture.

Channing's Baltimore sermon stood well within the liberal tradition Buckminster had so brilliantly espoused in Boston a decade earlier. The position Channing chose to defend represented nothing new

[3] Brown, *Always Young*, pp. 115–23.

[4] See James King Morse, *Jedidiah Morse, a Champion of New England Orthodoxy* (New York: Columbia University Press, 1939), pp. 121–49.

[5] Boston: Wells and Lilly, 1815. Morse had persuaded Jeremiah Evarts to review his pirated publication for the *Panoplist*.

to those familiar with the New England theological scene. Fundamentally he attacked the creedal and theological science of Calvinism on the basis of a more scientific interpretation of Scripture. But never before had the liberal principles of biblical interpretation been so widely published. The adherents of orthodoxy could not ignore the liberal threat so clearly posed by the address.

Channing's sermon was based on the belief in the progress of the human race, a belief which, though a legacy of the enlightenment, had become peculiarly American. First and foremost, the Bible was rightly to be seen as a record of "God's successive revelations to mankind"; each successive revelation marked a new stage of progress from the "childhood of the human race." [6] As a corollary to this axiom, Channing felt that liberals could not attach equal importance to all books of the Bible. Each book must be judged on its own merits. Generally speaking, New Testament books were of greater authority than Old Testament books. But distinctions must be made even within the New Testament.

> Jesus Christ is the only master of Christians, and whatever he taught, either during his personal ministry or by his inspired Apostles, we regard as of divine authority, and profess to make the rule of our lives.[7]

Because Channing found the locus of inspiration in the Apostles rather than in scriptural writings, he could establish a canon within the canon in the same way that Locke, early German critics, and Buckminster had done before him.

Because Channing did not regard the biblical books as supernaturally inspired, he could truly say that the foremost principle of scriptural interpretation was the treatment of the Bible on the same basis as any other ancient writing. The Bible was the source of many "general truths," presumably those truths taught by Jesus and his inspired Apostles. But the particular historical context of the books and the idiosyncrasies of their authors were also a part of the Bible. The responsible interpreter of Scripture must separate the general truths

---

[6] Channing, "Unitarian Christianity," in *The Works of William E. Channing, D.D.* (Boston: American Unitarian Association, 1896), p. 367.

[7] "Unitarian Christianity," p. 367.

from their historical context. Otherwise, Channing cautioned, "we are constantly in danger of extending to all times and places what was of temporary and local application." [8]

The process of interpretation clearly demanded the use of reason. "Revelation is addressed to us as rational beings." [9] Reason must be used to select the proper meaning of a scriptural text within the context of the proper understanding of a writer's situation. Reason must be used to detect the "general strain of Scripture." Finally, reason must be used to harmonize Scripture with "the known character and will of God, and with the obvious and acknowledged laws of nature." [10]

This last use of reason, which presupposed a revelation outside Scripture by which scriptural revelation might be judged, represented a new departure for New England liberals, who until that time had defended their position almost entirely on biblical grounds. Channing pointed out that traditional Calvinists employed their powers of reasoning quite as much as did the Unitarians. He did not clearly perceive that the use of reason by the orthodox was founded on and confined within a theological tradition or that his own use of reason reflected the values of a developing biblical science.

As much as Channing might rely on the powers of human reason, he clearly appealed to the Bible as the primary standard of Christian religion. "God's wisdom is a pledge that whatever is necessary for *us,* and necessary for salvation is revealed [in Scripture] too plainly to be mistaken, and too consistently to be questioned." Since the days when Charles Chauncy debated with Jonathan Edwards, New England liberals had appealed to Scripture to substantiate their position. Channing stood firmly in that tradition. But by Channing's day the principles of scriptural interpretation had become much more sophisticated. His appeal to the Bible assumed that the Bible must first be interpreted through the proper modes of criticism before its statements could be accepted as authoritative for religious faith and practice.

[8] "Unitarian Christianity," p. 368.
[9] "Unitarian Christianity," p. 370.
[10] "Unitarian Christianity," p. 369.

The Baltimore sermon forcefully restated the liberal arguments against the orthodox. Channing's strictures against the "unscriptural doctrine of the Trinity" and the doctrine of the two natures of Christ were founded upon his view of Scripture. To be sure, Channing was not the best spokesman for the liberal critics, since biblical criticism never engaged his interest to any appreciable degree. But in the Baltimore sermon he adequately reflected the point of view of his colleagues so that some issues were made clear. To defeat the liberals on the battle lines that had been drawn, the conservatives would have to find some way of refuting the liberal view of the nature and authority of the Bible.

This seemed a task for which Moses Stuart was eminently qualified. In a series of letters published in 1819 Stuart undertook an orthodox refutation of Channing's arguments.[11]

It is immediately evident that, so far as the liberal conception of the Bible was concerned, Stuart misunderstood the Baltimore sermon. Stuart assumed that for the most part his and Channing's principles of scriptural interpretation were identical. He had accepted enough of the doctrine of progressive revelation to agree that the New Testament represented a more authoritative revelation for the Christian than the Old Testament. He did feel that Channing showed too little respect for the Old Testament, for, as he argued, much of the Old Testament consisted of unrepealed laws that were addressed to man as a moral being and were thus free from merely local and national application. The prophecies of the Old Testament that were fulfilled in the New and the devotional literature in the Hebrew Scriptures were, Stuart thought, an indispensable part of the Christian heritage.[12]

Curiously, Stuart did not urge against Channing the arguments for the canon of the Old Testament that he so forcefully presented

[11] Moses Stuart, *Letters to the Rev. Wm. E. Channing, Containing Remarks on His Sermon Recently Preached and Published at Baltimore* (Andover: Flagg and Gould, 1819). The work was reprinted as "Letters to Dr. Channing on the Trinity" in Moses Stuart, *Miscellanies* (Andover: Allen, Morrill, and Wardwell, 1846), pp. 3–215. Subsequent citations were taken from the 1846 edition.

[12] "Letters to Dr. Channing," pp. 7–13.

in his Andover classes. To demonstrate that Jesus and his Apostles had accepted the Old Testament would have been a telling argument against the liberals, who, with the exception of Everett, had not been willing to see in the teachings of Jesus anything but authoritative universal truths.

Perhaps Stuart did not feel compelled to muster so formidable an argument because he naively thought that Channing would readily agree with his own statement of the principles of scriptural interpretation. For Stuart the question of interpretation was simply: "What did the original writer mean to convey?" [13] To answer this question, the biblical scholar ought to treat the Bible as he would any other ancient book, employing the proper grammatical and literary tools. But, once the interpretative questions have been answered, the Bible is no longer like any other writing: "It is authoritative. It is orthodoxy in the highest sense of the word; and everything which differs from it, which modifies it, which fritters it away, is *heterodoxy,* is heresy. . . ." [13] And this ultimate authority inheres in every single text of Scripture. In Stuart's terse maxim: "The decision of one text . . . is as authoritative as that of a thousand." [14]

"I hope you will agree, without hesitation, to these remarks," Stuart wrote.[14] He entertained a naive hope. Channing had quite clearly stated that before one text could be admitted as authoritative it must agree with the general spirit of Scripture, belong to the body of universal truth taught by Jesus and his Apostles, and coincide with what is generally known about God and the laws of nature. For Channing the question of interpretation was not merely, "What did the original writer mean to convey," but also, "Did the idea which the writer meant to convey have validity for all times and ages, or does it apply to the local, temporal situation only?"

Stuart was equally mistaken about his and Channing's use of reason. Thinking he had found common ground with his opponent, he wrote, "I am confident, that I admit as fully as you do or can do the *proper office* of reason, in the whole matter of religion. . . ." [13] For Stuart, the proper function of reason was to demonstrate that the Bi-

[13] "Letters to Dr. Channing," p. 11.
[14] "Letters to Dr. Channing," p. 43.

ble was the inspired word of God on the basis of its authenticated miracles, fulfilled prophecies, and ethical teachings. The doctrines and facts found within Scripture, even though beyond human reason, were to be accepted on God's authority.[15] Both Channing and Stuart accepted the validity of reason, but they used the word in different contexts. Channing was the child of enlightenment: he used reason over Scripture to distinguish the word of God, those "eternal universal truths," from the word of man. Stuart was the child of New England Puritanism: he used reason only to substantiate the authority of all Scripture.

Since Channing and Stuart did not share a common understanding about the nature of biblical interpretation, their discussion about the Trinity and the doctrine of the two natures of Christ was necessarily inconclusive. Channing was certain that no biblical author possessed sufficient philosophical acuity to distinguish accurately between "persons" and "being," as Trinitarians were forced to do.

> So entirely do the Scriptures abstain from stating the Trinity, that when our opponents would insert it into their creeds and doxologies, they are compelled to leave the Bible, and to invent forms of words altogether unsanctioned by Scriptural phraseology. That a doctrine so strange, so liable to misapprehension, so fundamental as this is said to be left so undefined and unprotected, to be made out by inference, and to be hunted through distant and detached parts of Scripture,—this is a difficulty which, we think, no ingenuity can explain.[16]

The inference of the Trinitarian formula from Scripture violated

---

[15] "[T]he sole office of reason in respect to them [Scriptures] is to act as the *interpreter* of Revelation, and not in any case as a *legislator*." "Letters to Dr. Channing," p. 10. In the 1846 edition Stuart noted that since 1819 he had realized that he had misunderstood Channing's position. In a footnote to the passage quoted above he added: "It is evident from the later writings of Dr. Channing, that he admitted the divine authority of the Old Testament only in a very limited and qualified sense. Of the New Testament he would doubtless have said: 'It *contains* the word of God;' so much is admitted to be authoritative, as agrees with our views of what is reasonable; in the second case, the Scripture is acknowledged as *the only rule of faith and practice.*" "Letters to Dr. Channing," pp. 10, 11.

[16] "Unitarian Christianity," p. 372.

Channing's principle that anything necessary for rational men and their salvation must be revealed consistently and plainly.[17]

To Channing it was unreasonable to suppose that the authors of the New Testament had conceived that God was three persons in one being while Christ was two beings in one person. He maintained that passages of the New Testament which seemed to describe Jesus as divine should be understood metaphorically or hyperbolically.[18] Human reason could discern that "the inferiority of Christ [to God] pervades the New Testament" and that he was consistently seen as distinct from the Father.[19] Jesus must be seen as having one nature, for "it is one of the most established and obvious principles of criticism, that language is to be explained according to the known properties of the subject to which it is applied." [18]

Because Stuart saw the Bible as an inspired unity that taught truths beyond the grasp of human reason, he contended that if one biblical author represented Jesus as God and another represented Jesus as man, Jesus must unite both beings in his person. Otherwise the authority of the Bible is undermined.

> The passages which seem to imply his inferiority to God, I find to be capable of explanation without doing violence to the language, by the obvious fact that he has two natures united, which the sacred writers seem to me so plainly to inculcate. In this way I find one consistent whole. I save the laws of exegesis. I admit, indeed, on the authority of revelation, doctrines which natural religion never taught; *but why should not a revelation teach something which natural religion did not?*
>
> Here then I take my stand. *I abide by the simple declarations of the New Testament writers, interpreted by the common laws of language.* Such views as I take, seem to me to reconcile all the seeming discrepancies of description in regard to Christ, without doing violence to the language of any particular passage. I can believe, and do believe, that the sacred writers are consistent, without any explanation but such as the laws of interpretation admit and require.[20]

[17] "Unitarian Christianity," p. 370.
[18] "Unitarian Christianity," p. 375.
[19] "Unitarian Christianity," p. 374.
[20] Stuart, "Letters to Dr. Channing," p. 171.

Similarly, Stuart maintained that if Jesus Christ and the Holy Spirit are spoken of as possessing attributes of divinity, the doctrine of the Trinity must be true, or the Bible has no authority.[21]

So little did Stuart understand Channing's radical departure from the orthodox understanding of biblical interpretation that he asked,

> How can it be explained, then, supposing that you and I are both seeking after truth, and that both adopt for substance the same maxims of interpretation, that we should differ so widely in the results that flow from the application of these principles? [22]

Stuart suspected that Channing had betrayed his reverence for Scripture by trusting too completely the powers of reason. Such a trust of reason had already led German critics into the chaos of infidelity, and Stuart gloomily prophesied that Channing's disciples would eventually follow the same disastrous course.

> I am well satisfied, that the course of reasoning in which you have embarked, and the principles by which you explain away the divinity of the Saviour, must eventually lead most men who approve them to the conclusion, that the Bible is not of divine origin, and does not oblige us to belief or obedience. I do not aver, that they will certainly lead *you* there. The remains of your former education and belief may still serve to guard you against the bolder conclusions of some of your brethren, who have not been placed under instruction such as you enjoyed in early life.[23]

Channing did not reply to Stuart's letters. Subsequent editions of the Baltimore sermon contained an appendix in which Channing

[21] Stuart, "Letters to Dr. Channing," p. 23.

[22] Stuart, "Letters to Dr. Channing," p. 13.

[23] Stuart, "Letters to Dr. Channing," pp. 175–76. Stuart describes the German heresey on pp. 176–92. He recorded his debt to the German critics, but held them to be fundamentally subversive of Christianity (p. 182). Although he did not think that the issue was important for Channing in 1819, he did not see how the Unitarians could fail eventually to follow the Germans to their logical conclusion and abandon the defense of the divine authenticity of the Bible (pp. 182–84). The charge that Unitarianism would lead to greater heresies was a popular argument of the orthodox. See C. H. Faust, "The Background of the Unitarian Opposition to Transcendentalism," *Modern Philology,* XXXV (1938), 297–307.

gave his exegesis of some portions of Scripture, but he made no attempt to show how Stuart had misunderstood the liberal conception of the authority of the Bible.[24] It must be remembered that Channing had no taste for theological polemics because he did not want to sunder New England Congregationalism. Furthermore, Channing himself was not a biblical scholar, and it may well be that he failed to understand the full significance of the liberal position he had defended in Baltimore.

Channing's silence after Stuart's counter-attack did not arise from indifference. Later, in a letter to Andrews Norton, Channing referred to Stuart as "a vain & rash man" whose pamphlet misrepresented the thesis of the Baltimore sermon. Nevertheless, Channing explained "so great is my desire to purify controversy from personalities that I incline to let him off as easily as consists with self respect."[25]

It is likely that Channing was responsible for Andrews Norton's joining the pamphlet battle. Curiously, Channing had recently opposed Norton's appointment to a Harvard professorship. But Norton was ever eager to join against the orthodox. In a letter to Norton, Channing urged that he study a pamphlet he had recently received. Channing continued:

> I have no desire whatever that an answer should be written from my vindication. The single question would be what the general interest of religion requires. The controversy should have as little to. do with individuals as possible. It is one of the chief wiles of party to mix up extraneous considerations with subjects of debate, to turn the publick mind from the true point of discussion. Even if I were in danger of suffering, I would rather suffer than have the attention of the people occupied with me. Besides, it is not impossible that I have in some respects erred and an honest man ought not to encumber himself so far with my cause. The object, I conceive should be to place in a clear light and set forth without exaggeration the differ-

[24] Channing, "Note for the Second Edition," in *A Sermon, Delivered at the Ordination of the Rev. Jared Sparks, to the Pastoral Care of the First Independent Church of Baltimore, May 5, 1819* (7th ed.; Boston: Cummings and Hilliard, 1821), pp. 45–51.

[25] Channing to Norton, 3 September 1832. Letter with the Norton Papers (MSS in the Houghton Library, Harvard University).

ences of the two systems, and to communicate as widely as possible a
tone of strength, independence, and courage to the publick mind,
that it may come to the subject without fear or prejudice. If, as we
apprehend, powerful instruments are in operation for enslaving and
palsifying the minds of men, they should be warned of their danger
and made to understand the signs of the times. In regard however to
the present pamphlet, I am not a judge, what nature it deserves. It
deserves none for its own sake—but the publick mind may render
some answer fit; or if not, the occasion may be a good one for drawing
attention to some important views. The question is who shall undertake [it], if any one must. . . .[26]

This veiled invitation was enough to move Norton.

Norton's defense of the Baltimore sermon was published in two
review articles which appeared in the *Christian Disciple* of 1819.[27]
The first article passed almost unnoticed by contemporaries and historians; the second, later published separately as a pamphlet entitled
*A Statement of Reasons for Not Believing the Doctrines of Trinitar-
ians Respecting the Nature of God, and the Person of Christ*, achieved
immediate and lasting fame.[28]

Although the major portion of Norton's first review was devoted
to demonstrating the logical inconsistencies of the orthodox doctrine
of the Trinity and Christology, he made some attempt to reassert the
primary importance of the biblical question. "In a controversy respecting any doctrine, which is to be established, or disproved, by the
words of Scripture," he wrote, "it is of primary importance to settle
correct principles of interpretation. . . ."[29] And Norton suspected
that Stuart could not actually agree as fully with Channing on the
rules of interpretation as he seemed to assume. Norton supposed that
Stuart's difficulty arose from his "loose" and "inconsistent" conceptions about the nature of the Bible.

[26] Channing to Norton, Wednesday, May 2. The letter designates no year,
but the content and context place it after the appearance of Stuart's pamphlet
and before Norton's rejoinder, hence 1819. The letter seems to fit no other
controversy.

[27] Norton, "Review of Moses Stuart's *Letters to the Rev. Wm. E. Channing*" *Christian Disciple*, N.S., I (1819), 316–33, 370–431.

[28] Boston: Wells and Lilly, 1819.

[29] Norton, "Review," p. 319.

Norton offered two examples of Stuart's looseness and inconsistency. Stuart had written that rules of biblical interpretation were derived from the process of investigating the meaning of ancient writings. Norton objected that a process is governed by prior rules and is not a general principle from which rules may be derived. Stuart had argued that rules of interpretation must be employed because a biblical writer wished to be understood by his contemporaries. Norton objected that this was a slender foundation upon which to erect a biblical science.[30] This was an extremely weak statement for a man who had contended that the methodology of scriptural interpretation represented a crucial difference between the liberals and conservatives, and who had argued for his Harvard appointment on the basis of his demonstrated ability to urge the critical interpretation of the Scripture against the uninformed methods of the orthodox. The cutting edge of Channing's forthright presentation was considerably dulled by such an ineffective counter-attack.

Norton's second review article, the more famous *Statement of Reasons,* shifted the area of contention from the question of biblical interpretation to the question of the logical possibility of the Trinitarian formulas and the Christological dogmas of orthodoxy.[31] Norton abandoned the stated project of his first review of giving a direct refutation of Stuart's letters. Such an attempt would involve "pointing out errors, inconsistences [sic], and rash and unfounded assertions . . . [which] would serve to distract our attention . . . from the real question at issue."[32] Channing had made the question of scriptural interpretation the central issue of the controversy. Buckminster, and even Norton at an earlier period, had followed the same course. But in the *Statement of Reasons* Norton clearly felt that the "real question" was the question of the Trinity.

Only twice in the second review did Norton allude to the princi-

[30] Norton, "Review," p. 320.
[31] This change in tactics was Norton's idea. He wrote to John Gorham Palfrey: "I am writing an enormous review—out of all compass, out of all reasonable compass, Sir John—not of Stuart, but about the doctrine of the Trinity." Norton to Palfrey, 1819; no month or day given. Letter is with the Norton Papers.
[32] *Statement of Reasons,* p. 3.

ples of scriptural criticism. First he offered his own understanding of the basis of interpretation.

> The art of interpretation derives its origin from the *intrinsic ambiguity of language.* . . . A very large proportion of sentences, *considered in themselves, merely in respect to the words of which they are composed,* are capable of expressing not one meaning only, but two or more different meanings. . . .[33]

Second, Norton proposed a simple rule to overcome the ambiguity of language in the interpretation of the New Testament.

> *It is necessary to have just notions of the intellectual and moral character of our Saviour and his apostles, and of the circumstances under which they wrote or spoke.*[34]

In passing, Norton depreciated German biblical scholarship, contending that it had contributed nothing new to the art of interpretation. Norton found it surprising that the orthodox Stuart could find anything of value in the writings of such heretics.[34]

During the course of 1819 the liberal movement within New England Congregationalism had undergone a dramatic and significant change. Up to that time the liberals had considered themselves within the main body of New England Christianity. They had attempted to reform New England theology by appealing to a more scientific interpretation of Scripture. The doctrine of the Trinity had been discarded, not because it was logically distasteful but because it was unscriptural. Men like Buckminster urged their colleagues to discard metaphysical theology and master instead the biblical science of continental scholars. The repristination of Christianity, they believed, would follow as a natural result.

The orthodox repeatedly attempted to force the liberal party to confess that they stood *outside* New England Congregationalism. Until 1819 this attempt met with little success, for the liberals continually referred to the common adherence to scriptural authority on the part of both factions. Conservatives had no spokesman adequately versed in biblical studies to undertake the task of discrediting the methods by which the liberals derived the doctrines that all the orthodox con-

[33] *Statement of Reasons*, pp. 38–39.
[34] *Statement of Reasons*, p. 43.

sidered heretical. Orthodox Calvinists could only decry the theological results of the new biblical interpretation.

Moses Stuart could understand that in Germany the question of biblical interpretation and the authority of Scripture was the crucial question, but he could not see the centrality of that same question in America, even when stated so clearly as in Channing's Baltimore sermon. Rather than replying to Channing as a biblical scholar, he chose to respond as a theologian, objecting to Channing's results rather than to his method.

Prior to 1819 Andrews Norton had considered the biblical question to be the central issue between liberals and conservatives. However, even as editor of the *General Repository,* he demonstrated the sectarian spirit that had alienated Channing. Norton was more willing than other liberals to remain outside the mainstream of the New England religious tradition and to erect a liberal orthodoxy he could defend against all opponents. In the debates of 1819 he abandoned the issue that affected the whole of New England theology—the question of biblical authority—and offered an apology for the distinctive liberal doctrine of the unity of God. In offering the distinctive doctrines of the liberals, Norton was engaging in theological formulation, which the older liberals had eschewed. Under his leadership religious liberals in New England were being transformed from a party within Congregationalism to a distinctive denomination outside Congregationalism. Significantly, Norton played a prominent role in the organization of the American Unitarian Society in 1825, while Channing, the traditional liberal, declined its presidency. Norton accomplished what the orthodox could not: the exclusion of the liberals from New England Congregationalism. In the charge and counter-charge that followed the Baltimore sermon, the original battle lines between liberal and orthodox had been circumvented.[35]

[35] Traditional interpretations of the Baltimore sermon and its aftermath have followed Stuart and Norton in supposing that the crucial questions concerned Trinitarian and Christological doctrines. Frank H. Foster, in *A Genetic History of the New England Theology* (Chicago: University of Chicago Press, 1907), supposes that Stuart emerged the decisive victor in the debate (pp. 299, 302). Foster overlooks the fact that Stuart's exegesis represented the labor of a theologian who assumed that the Bible was so infallibly inspired that it could contain no contradictions, and whose authors had access to truth

available to no other men. Without these assumptions, which Channing had explicitly denied, his exegesis carried little weight. Stuart acted as a theologian, not as a biblical scholar; he failed to grapple with the issue of biblical authority raised by Channing's sermon. Channing could not be defeated by exegesis of particular passages of Scripture because Channing would not admit that all Scripture was equally binding on Christian theology.

Joseph Haroutunian, in *Piety Versus Moralism* (New York: Holt, 1932), disputes this. "Professor Andrews Norton of Harvard was easily the equal of Stuart of Andover. Being well versed in 'Sacred Literature,' he was able to show that certain ways of construing Scripture passages lead to downright absurdity" (p. 202). Like Foster, he fails to note Norton's shift in position: Norton's reviews attempted to establish the logical absurdity of the Trinitarian theology rather than continuing Channing's discussion about the nature of biblical authority.

The important shift in the liberal position was noted by an anonymous orthodox reviewer. He pointed out that between 1815 and 1826 Unitarians had passed through three phases in their attack on the orthodox. "Unitarians began now [the author means about 1815, although he should have dated the movement earlier], in their periodical journals and in conversation, openly to state and advocate their opinions, and to oppose and denounce those of the Orthodox. The weapons of attack and defence they employed, were chiefly derived from *Biblical literature*. Erroneous readings, mistranslations, and wrong interpretations, were the charges perpetually preferred against the doctrines of the Orthodox, and the scriptural arguments by which they were maintained. The Orthodox, it was alleged, had too superficial an acquaintance with the original languages of the Bible, and with those kindred dialects which have thrown so much light upon scriptural phraseology, and their investigations of the composition and history of the Bible were too limited, to ascertain what portions of the received text were genuine, and what were the doctrines really taught in those portions. Had they a little more learning, especially the learning requisite for a successful criticism of the Scriptures, they would, generally, there was no doubt, become Unitarians. The study of Biblical criticism was, moreover, beginning to be cultivated among them; and the result, it was confidently and often predicted, would be, a rapid disappearance of the antiquated doctrines of Orthodoxy." The author continued by describing Stuart's refutation of Channing, "conducted almost entirely on the principles of Biblical criticism." In his opinion, Stuart had never been answered. Instead, "the trial of Orthodoxy was now transferred to another tribunal, that of *philosophy*. Its doctrines were declared to be irrational and absurd, wholly inconsistent with the perfections of God, and the freedom and accountability of man." The current phase the orthodox reviewer identified as that of arguing that Unitarianism tended to produce better morality. *Review of Dr. Channing's Discourse, Preached at the Dedication of the Second Congregational Unitarian Church, New York, December 7, 1826* (Boston: Hilliard, Gray, Little, and Wilkins, 1827).

CHAPTER V

LIBERAL ENTRENCHMENT
Andrews Norton: 1820–1847

IN the controversy created by Channing's Baltimore sermon of
1819, Andrews Norton had veered from the course established by
earlier New England liberals. Rather than urging a critical study of
the Bible to reform New England theology, he had preferred to defend the distinctive liberal doctrines of the unity of God and the simple nature of Christ. Nevertheless, in his lectures as Dexter Professor
of Sacred Literature at Harvard he demonstrated a deep indebtedness
to the scholarly tradition initiated by Buckminster. At his inaugura-
tion as Dexter Professor in 1819 Norton proposed that students in
divinity might rediscover the "very striking evidence of the truth of
our religion" if they would first remove the "accumulated rubbish"
and the "technical theology" that had concealed simple scriptural
truth.[1] Norton, in his typically effusive style, promised those enrolled in his course that he would "strip away the mistletoe and ivy
which have covered the tree of life." [2]

Norton's lectures at Harvard were not nearly so ambitious in scope
as were Stuart's at Andover. In the decade before 1830, when Norton
retired from active teaching, his lectures on biblical criticism were actually limited to the subject of hermeneutics. While he recognized
the leadership of German scholarship in biblical studies, he had little
respect for what he regarded as "licentious," "extravagant," and

[1] *Inaugural Discourse Delivered before the University in Cambridge,
August 10, 1819* (Cambridge: Hilliard and Metcalf, 1819), p. 15.
[2] Lectures, V (IVa), (MSS in the Harvard University Archives; microfilm copy in Union Theological Seminary Library). Apparently Norton divided his series differently through the years of his teaching; where applica-
ble, both numbers of the particular lecture have been cited.

"untenable speculations" of German scholars.[3] Unlike Stuart, who thought his students should be aware of critical opinions even when erroneous, Norton chose to ignore the German heresies. By confining his lectures to the subject of hermeneutics he avoided questions of canonicity, historicity, and authorship.

It is not surprising that Emerson called Norton "the old tyrant of the Cambridge Parnassus," and Carlyle referred to him as the "Unitarian Pope."[4] Norton clearly considered himself the intellectual leader of New England liberalism. From the Dexter Chair at Harvard students of divinity could learn all the necessary principles of biblical criticism and subsequently convey them to their congregations. Andrews Norton stood at the head of this hierarchical structure, and if many lacked the skill and time to pursue biblical studies competently, they could rely on his authority.

The first task Norton undertook in his lectures was that of explaining how the New Testament had been so distorted that it could be made to support erroneous dogmatic systems. Norton felt that the church fathers had initiated the tradition of distorted scriptural interpretation, for they understood neither the Jewish origins of Christianity nor the historical context in which Christian truth had originally been taught. Consequently they steered the church away from its intended course and wedded scriptural truth with alien philosophy. Since Gentile Christians were responsible for the transmission of Christianity, the "extravagant errors" of the fathers permeated the whole church.[5]

---

[3] *Inaugural Discourse*, p. 35. Norton's distrust of German scholarship eventually became so pronounced that he would not allow his son to learn the language "for fear that it would corrupt his Unitarianism." Henry A. Pochman, *German Culture in America* (Madison: University of Wisconsin Press, 1961), p. 561 n. 439.

[4] Cited by Conrad Wright "The Early Period," in *The Harvard Divinity School*, George Huntston Williams, ed. (Boston: Beacon, 1954), p. 49. When Norton told his class that "it is the lot of the great majority of mankind, to receive the most of their opinions relating to the higher branches of knowledge upon authority," he clearly had himself in mind. Lectures, IV.

[5] Lectures, IV. This interpretation of early church history shows the influence of Joseph Priestley's *History of the Corruptions of Christianity* (1782).

The reformers, Norton felt, had made an important forward step in returning to the study of the Scriptures. But, like the early fathers, they misunderstood the historical context in which the Scriptures were written. They mistakenly accepted the Bible as God's very word and consequently had based all their theology on the proposition that the Bible was the infallible word of God. That proposition could not be rationally demonstrated.[6]

The history of biblical interpretation was important to Norton, for he believed that the errors of the fathers and reformers had determined the shape of Protestant orthodoxy in New England. The persistence of error in scriptural interpretation originated in the fact that most people received religious education before they could read the Bible critically. Subsequently, when the common man read the Scriptures he interpreted them in the ways in which he was accustomed to think, not recognizing "that the meaning of the Sc[riptures] like the meaning of all other ancient writings is often to be discovered only by study and attention."[7] This eisegetical bias was compounded by the assumption that the Bible was the revelation of God, a book written for all men in all times. On the basis of this assumption, Christian dogmaticians quoted isolated verses as propositions eternally true, guaranteed by the authority of God.[8]

In opposition to this position, Norton located the authoritative revelation of God in "the great truths of religion" to be found within the Bible.[9] These "great truths" were embedded in a framework that reflected the local and temporary situation of the biblical writers. Their meaning was disguised in a peculiar idiom and style. With no thought of posterity, the biblical authors had attempted to convey these truths to a contemporary and relatively naive audience. The preaching of Jesus and the teaching of the Apostles reported in the New Testament had been accommodated to the ignorance and prejudices of their original audience.[8]

The task of the scriptural exegete, as Norton saw it, was to re-

[6] Lectures, VII (8).
[7] Lectures, X (IX).
[8] Lectures, 6.
[9] Lectures, VII (8).

cover the "great truths" that formed the authoritative revelation of God and to use them to restore Christianity to its original purity. Norton's Harvard lectures could provide the critical tools essential to this task: for dogmatic presuppositions and prejudices the student was to substitute a critical understanding of the Jewish world during the Christian era and a thorough knowledge of the ideas of the biblical period.[10] In addition, Norton would guide his students to an appreciation of the inherent ambiguity of all language and thus help them to overcome rigid literalism in the science of interpretation.

Norton underestimated the difficulty of recreating the historical background of the biblical writings. His course of earlier lectures as Dexter Lecturer had been concerned with this problem and reveals the nature of his oversimplification. He regarded the Gospels primarily as historical documents, and thought that, with the help of the Old Testament and a knowledge of classical antiquity, an intelligent man could accurately recreate the historical background of the New Testament. Consequently, he devoted little effort to this problem in his later lectures. Since the goal of his studies was to separate eternal truths from historical background, he could easily employ his understanding of eternal truth to discover matters he regarded as historical fact. On this basis, and because Norton did not include a doctrine of Satan in his beliefs, he concluded that the sayings of Jesus regarding Satan were in fact accommodations to the prejudices of the Jews.

Norton's delineation of the task of scriptural interpretation appealed to the reforming interests of liberal Christians. He told his students:

> [The interpreter of Scripture] must leave behind him and forget our modern doctrines, and prejudices, and associations. He must make himself familiar and contemporary with men . . . [of] eighteen centuries ago. . . .[11]

But it was easier to state the case for a presuppositionless exegesis than to act upon it. As long as irrational or undesirable teachings of Jesus and the Apostles could be dismissed as accommodation to the

---

[10] Lectures, IV, X.
[11] Lectures, VI.

condition and prejudices of an earlier age, no tenet held by the rationalistic liberals could be corrected by biblical revelation.

The course of hermeneutical lectures Norton delivered at Harvard also provided him with a fine opportunity for the discussion of one of his favorite topics, the ambiguity of language. In the lectures Norton attempted to formulate general principles of interpretation that applied to all literature. The examples he cited were as likely to be drawn from Burke, Cowper, and Johnson as from the Bible.

Norton conceived the revelation of God to be conceptual rather than verbal. He believed the final goal of the biblical interpreter to be the recovery of the true conceptions in the Bible and the application of them to religion. Obviously he would have to master the biblical languages, understand the historical context of the writings, and fathom the writer's ideas. But the use of these tools could not overcome the inherent problem of language itself: "Language . . . is a very imperfect instrument for expressing thoughts." [12]

Norton attempted to establish two propositions concerning the nature of language.

> 1. That the meaning of the words wh[ich] constitute a sentence, supposing us guided in ascertaining their meaning only by the words themselves, is very frequently uncertain and indeterminate, or altogether inexplicable; or to state the same thing differently, that the words which constitute a sentence are often when considered in themselves either inexpressive of any distinct meaning, or capable of being taken in two or more different significations, each or all of which, they are equally adapted to express.
>
> 2. That the meaning of language therefore is frequently to be determined by a regard to a variety of considerations; and that in order to ascertain it, a process, or an act of reasoning is necessary, which is sometimes obvious enough for the mind to take cognizance of it, but much more frequently so rapid as to escape observation. [13]

In expounding these propositions, Norton demonstrated that some language, rather than directly expressing truth, was "intended to

[12] Lectures, 10. Norton was probably indebted to the Scottish commonsense philosophers, particularly Stewart and Campbell, for this idea of language.
[13] Lectures, X (IX).

produce an effect upon the imagination or feeling . . . coincident with the truth." [14] Many sentences were "true only in relation to some certain subject." [14] The interpreter must also consider the language of passion, produced by a "strongly excited" mind, and marked by hyperbole and bold figures that might actually be false but were intended to bring associated truth into view by appealing to the imagination. As an illustration Norton cited the saying of Jesus that he had not come to bring peace but a sword, and Jeremiah's "the heart is desperately wicked." [15]

Employing the considerations he had urged, Norton was confident that the intelligent interpreter could arrive at the truth contained in a sentence.

> Considering the moral and intellectual character of him by whom they were employed, and the state of things by wh[ich] his mind was affected at the time of speaking or writing, we judge that meaning to be the true one, which we judge that a person of such character, in such a state of things, would be most disposed to express. We adopt the meaning because it is as we say reasonable, and reject another because it is unreasonable. . . . We do not intend by . . . [these terms] that either meaning is reasonable or unreasonable considered in itself; for we often understand an author as expressing an idea wh[ich] appears to us as inconsistent with truth and good sense; but what we do intend, is, that considering the character of the author, his opinions and feeling; and the circumstances in wh[ich] he was placed, it is reasonable to suppose such a meaning to be that wh[ich] it was his purpose to express. In order to understand the words of another, we assimilate as far as possible our minds to his, and enter into his situation; and we then understand his language in that sense, in wh[ich], with his character, in his circumstances, and using language with the same license or the same restriction wh[ich] he does, we should ourselves employ his words.[14]

Significantly, Norton noted that before his program of exegesis could be employed it was necessary to ascertain that the author whose works were examined was "a rational man, or in other words, a man of common sense, that in the conformation of his understanding he resem-

[14] Lectures, X.
[15] Lectures, XIV.

bles the rest of mankind. . . ." [16] For all his insistence on the necessity of understanding the historical context of biblical writings, Norton did not function as an historical critic. He continually assumed a non-critical historiography in supposing that men of the first and second century shared a rational view of the world with men of the nineteenth century.

In his Harvard lectures Norton functioned much more adequately as a critic of the orthodox than as a pioneer of a new liberal biblical science. He pointedly demonstrated the fallacies involved in regarding the Bible as a source of doctrinal texts, but his understanding of the historical influence that had shaped the Bible was over-simplified. His theory of language pointed to a great inadequacy in the theory of verbal inspiration, but he failed to demonstrate the use of his literary technique as a means of biblical research. Like the orthodox, Norton located the authoritative revelation of God in the Bible; he had no doubt that with the use of his reason he could discover religious conceptions as binding upon the liberals as the literal propositions used by the orthodox.

Norton resigned his Harvard professorship in 1830. He had married a woman of wealth and wished to devote all his time to his studies. Since 1819 he had been involved in a work on the "genuineness of the Gospels," and even earlier had sought Bancroft's advice and aid in procuring German books while the latter was still a student in Europe.[17] Norton was a painstaking scholar, and, although he had thought he would finish his study for publication within a few months, the first of the three volumes of *The Genuineness of the Gospels* did not appear until 1837.[18]

In his work on the Gospels Norton attempted to substantiate and maintain the position originally espoused by John Locke. Like Locke, Norton was willing to assume a critical attitude toward the Bible

[16] Lectures, X.

[17] See letters to Bancroft, 11 August 1818; 1 December 1818; 12 January 1819; 24 May 1819. Norton correspondence is with the Norton Papers (MSS in the Houghton Library, Harvard University).

[18] *The Evidences of the Genuineness of the Gospels* (3 vols.; I, Boston: American Stationer's Company, John B. Russell, 1837; II, III, Cambridge: John Owen, 1844).

simply because he was certain that the essence of Christianity could be found in the Gospels. Locke had played a major role in early German biblical studies, but by Norton's day German scholars were turning their critical attention to the Gospels. Lessing had published the works on the Gospels of the rationalist Paulus, who had dared to suggest that the reported miracles were merely exaggerations of natural events by credulous followers of Jesus. Gabler had continued along this line. And Eichhorn, the dean of German critics, had suggested that the four Gospels were second-century recensions of one original Gospel and therefore could not be relied upon as accurate historical accounts of the life of Jesus.

Norton considered the critical work of Locke a good place for American liberals to call a halt. He designed his work on the Gospels to defend an entrenched liberalism. His chief opponents were the Germans, particularly Eichhorn, for although there had been great interest in their work, German critics of the Gospels had no American disciples. Nevertheless, Moses Stuart had predicted that American Unitarians would eventually follow German rationalism; Norton's work was designed to arrest any tendency in that direction. He undertook to demonstrate that the Gospels presented an authentic account of Jesus Christ, who as God's messenger established the basis of true religion. If this case could be proved, all the new critics of Germany could be ignored, and American liberalism could be stabilized on a Lockean foundation.

Norton's *Genuineness of the Gospels* attempted to prove that the four canonical Gospels were written by the authors to whom they had been attributed and that they had remained "essentially the same" as the original autographs. The work was particularly directed against Eichhorn's *Einleitung in das Neue Testament,* in which he had proposed his theory that there had been originally but one primitive gospel, from which the four recognized Gospels were subsequently derived. Norton could not accept the hypothesis of an original gospel that preceded the Gospels. Such a document, had it ever existed, would have been supported by the authority of the Apostles, and the Christian church could not have allowed it to perish. Nor could Norton find any trace of an original gospel within the synoptics; the style of each Gospel writer was too individualistic, and the correspondences between them did not yield any connected history of Christ. Finally, Norton accepted the external testimony that established the eyewitness Matthew as the author of the first Gospel, and Mark and Luke, companions of the Apostles, as the authors of the other two synoptics. Authorities such as Matthew, Mark, and Luke needed no recourse to an anonymous primitive gospel.[19]

Norton could see no literary interdependence within the Gospels at all. Common material could not be explained on the basis of any rational principle of selection, nor could one account for the variations within parallel passages, for those variations made no improvement in the writing.[20] He attributed similarities in the Gospels to a common subject matter and thought the four Gospels could be harmonized by rational principles. In denying the validity of an original-gospel hypothesis, in rejecting any theory of the literary interdependence of the Gospels, and in refusing to separate the three synoptics from John, Norton was resisting the most fundamental trends in modern New Testament scholarship. The influential Eichhorn and Griesbach had devised these important critical hypotheses, but their theories did not suit Norton's purpose.

Norton advanced four basic arguments in support of his case for the genuineness of the Gospels. First, he noted that a comparison of extant New Testament manuscripts indicated a dependence on a text fixed early in the history of the church. Second, the Gospels, written in a Greek dialect peculiar to Palestine, must have been written before the division between the Jewish and Gentile churches. Third, the testimony of the church fathers indicated the early existence of four Gospels of apostolic authority. And finally, the Gnostics had supported their heretical doctrines only by appealing to the four canonical Gospels.

Eichhorn had supposed that an original gospel of the first century had been expanded and corrupted in a process of recension throughout the second century. Toward the end of the second century four of many recensions were accepted by the church, given their present

[19] Norton, *Genuineness*, I, clix–clxi.
[20] Norton, *Genuineness*, I, cxxxi, cxxxii.

titles, and ultimately recognized as the only canonical Gospels. Norton contended that if the text of the Gospels had been as fluid as Eichhorn had supposed, extant manuscripts should have contained many more variant readings than was the case.[21] Further, Norton could not feel that any group of men could be so dull as to fail to preserve the text of sacred writings or to feel free to make alterations and additions to a sacred book. Finally, had the church agreed at the end of the second century to accept four recensions as authoritative, it would certainly have been mentioned in the writings of the period. Such a decision would have been difficult, for each community would have insisted on its own Gospel as authoritative above the others.[22]

These were effective arguments against Eichhorn's position, but Norton would not stop there. He even denied Griesbach's theory of textual families, because he could find no mention of such recensions in ancient authors, and it served his purpose to consider that the text was established at an early date.[23] Since the days of Buckminster Griesbach had been regarded as an eminent authority by the liberal party, but Norton feared that the genuineness of the Gospels was threatened by his theories.

In Norton's day it was not known that the New Testament was written in *koinē*—the common Greek dialect of the Hellenistic world. Since the Greek of the New Testament differed from that of classical writings, it was thought that New Testament Greek was peculiar to Palestine. Therefore, Norton could argue that the Gospels must have originated in a period before the separation of the Jewish and Gentile churches, for, in his mind, no native Greek could have written in a Jewish dialect.[24]

[21] Norton knew of 670 manuscripts of the Gospels. "These different copies of the Gospels or parts of the Gospels, so numerous, so various in their character, so unconnected, offering themselves to notice in parts of the world so remote from each other, concur in giving us essentially the same text. Divide them into four classes, corresponding to the four Gospels, and it is evident, that those of each class are to be referred to one common source; that they are all copies more or less remote of the same original; that they all had one common text for their authority." *Genuineness*, I, 27–29.

[22] *Genuineness*, I, 37 ff., 169.

[23] *Genuineness*, I, xxxii.

[24] *Genuineness*, I, 82–84.

Norton next turned to the external testimony of early Christian writers. His principal witness was Justin Martyr, but before his testimony could be accepted Norton had to overcome three of Eichhorn's objections: 1) Justin nowhere refers to the Gospels by name; 2) his quotations have little verbal coincidence with the Gospels; 3) Justin used quotations not found in the canonical Gospels. To the first objection Norton replied that Justin had written for a heathen audience, to whom the names of the Gospel writers would have no significance. Rather than citing the proper names of the authors he gave them the greatest authority possible by referring to them simply as the "memoirs of apostles." To the second objection Norton replied that the fathers in general prefer to paraphrase and render the sense of a passage rather than to cite it verbatim. He noted that Justin's quotations from the Septuagint and from classical authors were most often paraphrased. To the third objection Norton replied that Justin may have taken some of his citations from an oral tradition, but that in any case the presence of quotations not found in canonical Gospels could not argue against Justin's having actually used those Gospels. Finally, to demonstrate his case Norton made a long list of parallel passages in Justin Martyr and the four Gospels.[25]

The writings of Justin were the earliest testimony of the genuineness of the Gospels that Norton could cite. However, he regarded it as highly significant that Origen, who had demonstrated a particular interest in textual studies, had accepted the four Gospels early in the second century.[26] Origen's testimony was substantiated by that of Clement of Alexandria and Irenaeus, among a host of other second-century writers. This combined testimony substantiated Norton's contention that during the second century the entire Christian community accepted the four Gospels as authentic productions of the apostolic age. Since the faith of the second-century Christian community depended upon the truth of the Gospels, those Christians could not have evaded any questions concerning the validity and genuineness of the accounts. They were fully capable of settling these questions, had there been any reason for doubting the authority and

[25] *Genuineness*, I, 181–239; ccvii–cclv.
[26] *Genuiness*, I, 68 ff.

genuineness of the Gospels. No supposition other than that the Gospels were indeed the products of the four evangelists whose names they bore could adequately account for the universal reception in the second-century Christian community.[27]

In addition to the proof that Norton found within the second-century Christian community, he thought that the writings of the heretical Gnostics also bore witness to the genuineness of the Gospels. In his typical painstaking manner he found it necessary to describe completely the features of the Gnostic Christians before drawing any testimony from them. Consequently, almost the whole of volumes two and three of his *magnum opus* dealt with a minute description, based on the works of early Christian writers, of the various Gnostic sects. The purpose of this long digression into Gnostic history was to validate Norton's statement that "the Gnostics had no other gospel-history than that which was common to them with the Catholic Christians and with ourselves. . . ."[28]

Norton supposed that had the Gnostics possessed any gospels more favorable to their heretical doctrine than the canonical four they would have employed them extensively against the Catholic Christians. Had this been the case, abundant evidence of the existence of other gospels would have persisted to Norton's day. Marcionites had their own canon of scripture, but it was an abridgement of the Catholic canon; they merely rejected some passages and books. But their final authority in matters of doctrine were books they held in common with the Catholic church.[29]

Two references by church fathers gave Norton considerable difficulty. Irenaeus had mentioned a gospel, current among Valentinian Gnostics, called the "Gospel of Truth." The common testimony revealed that the Valentinians accepted the four canonical Gospels, and although Irenaeus had stated that the heretics had more gospels than the Catholic Christians, Norton could say that they had only one

[27] *Genuineness*, I, 133 ff.

[28] *Genuineness*, III, 192.

[29] *Genuineness*, III, 209–11. Norton's guess was incorrect. In 1945 a large collection of Gnostic writings, including many "gospels," was discovered at Nag Hamadi in Egypt. See W. C. van Unnik, *Newly Discovered Gnostic Writings* ("Studies in Biblical Theology," No. 30 [London: SCM, 1960]).

more, and that this gospel, then, could not have conflicted with the four Gospels they had received in common with other Christians. Furthermore, Norton contended such a gospel might not have been a gospel in the true sense of the word, but quite probably contained a summary of the crucial doctrines of the Gospels. Finally, Norton conjectured that perhaps Irenaeus had made an honest mistake. The "true gospel" might have referred merely to "the true doctrines of the gospel," and not to a separate book of that name.[30]

But there was no doubt that the "Gospel According to the Egyptians" mentioned by Clement of Alexandria actually existed. Furthermore, it contained, to all appearances, a narrative of a conversation between Jesus and Salome not found in the canonical Gospels. Norton discredited the book: it was "an anonymous book," written in the "dark and mystical style" of Egypt, known by few writers. Probably it was not an historical account of Christ's ministry, but a textbook of Gnostic doctrines, which only incidentally contained an unknown saying of Jesus. Norton maintained that such an isolated and unimportant book could not be used against his supposition that the Gnostics had known, and recognized the authority of, only the four canonical Gospels.[31]

It is evident from the work Norton did on the Gnostic gospels that there was some confusion in his own mind about the nature of a gospel. Clearly, in his discussion of the Gnostics, Norton considered a gospel to be an historical account of the ministry of Jesus. Since he knew of no historical accounts possessed by the Gnostics that contradicted the history contained in the four Gospels, he felt assured that the Gnostic heretics testified to the genuineness of the Gospels. But Norton did not always consider the Gospels as histories. In his Harvard lectures he noted that the Gospels seemed more like memoranda written for contemporaries than histories written for posterity. Only Matthew, he thought, presented any kind of an historical chro-

[30] *Genuineness*, III, 223 ff. Norton should have given Irenaeus more credence. "The Gospel of Truth" was one of the Gnostic writings recovered at Nag Hamadi.

[31] *Genuineness*, III, 236 ff. The document Clement quoted has still not been recovered, although a gospel entitled "The Gospel According to the Egyptians" was in the Nag Hamadi find; van Unnik, *Gnostic Writings*, p. 12.

nology.[32] Furthermore, at times Norton considered the Gospels to have been composed upon a kerygmatic rather than on an historical foundation. The Gospels represented a presentation of the Apostles, who had felt free to rearrange materials from the life of Jesus according to the systematic and occasional needs of their preaching. This might even result in a change of meaning of the primitive words of Jesus.

> The apostles, familiar as they were with the words of their Master, and continually using them in their discourses, would often quote them separate from their original connexion. They would blend together those uttered at different times in relation to the same subject; and they would, likewise, naturally apply to new occasions his striking expressions and figurative language, so as sometimes to divert his words, more or less, from their primitive meaning, or, at least, their primary reference.[33]

Norton cited two examples of such rearrangement, first comparing Matthew 10:23–26 with Luke 12:57–59.

Matthew	*Luke*
So if you are offering your gift at the altar, and there remember that your brother has something against you, leave your gift there before the altar and go; first be reconciled to your brother, and then come and offer your gift. Make friends quickly with your accuser, while you are going with him to court, lest your accuser hand you	And why do you **not** judge for yourselves what is right? As you go with your accuser before the magistrate, make an effort to settle with him on the way, lest he drag you to the judge, and the judge hand you over to the officer, and the officer put you in prison. I tell you, you will never get out till you have paid the very last copper.

[32] Lectures, 6.
[33] Norton, *Genuineness,* I, clxxxvi–cxci.

> over to the judge,
> and the judge to the
> guard, and you be put
> in prison; truly, I
> say to you, you will
> never get out till
> you have paid the
> last penny.

Norton commented on the Matthean version:

> This is the conclusion of a passage in which our Saviour warns his followers, in the most solemn manner, against being angry without cause, and expressing ill-will to others even by injurious language. . . . He is to show his good will toward him [his brother] quickly, lest he should be called to suffer the full punishment of his offence.

On the Lucan account, he noted:

> Here our Saviour is represented as reproaching the bigoted Jews for the blindness to the character of the times, by which is meant to those proofs of a divine interposition that his ministry was continually affording. Even if these proofs were less striking, they might judge from themselves what it was right for them to do; which was to secure the favor of God, and to obtain from him pardon of their sins by reformation. Otherwise, they would be acting as one who should make no effort to propitiate his creditor (as he might do); and who, in consequence, should be condemned to imprisonment till the full amount of his debt was paid; that is, they would remain exposed to the full punishment of their sins.

From a comparison of the two passages, Norton concluded:

> It is true, that Jesus may have used the same, or similar words and figures, in different senses on different occasions. But, as regards this passage in Luke, there is not merely the fact, that the words are found in Matthew with another connexion and meaning; but the obscurity of the passage itself, the want of obvious adaptation of one part to another, and the difficulty in discovering the relations of the ideas, serve to show, that expressions have been brought together which were not originally connected.[34]

[34] Biblical quotations are from the Revised Standard Version. Norton's treatment may be found in *Genuineness,* I, clxxxix–cxci.

Norton treated the parallel passages Matthew 10:26–28 and Luke 8: 16–18 in a similar manner. In noting that Luke's change of context and scene had altered the meaning of the words of Jesus, he had perceived an important feature of the Gospels that could have revolutionized Gospel studies in his day.[35] But he was more concerned with finding solutions than with exploring problems. His valuable insights concerning the nature of the Gospels could do nothing to substantiate their genuineness.

In a manuscript published posthumously in 1855 Norton outlined what he regarded as "internal evidences" for the genuineness of the Gospels.[36] He posed the alternative that the Gospels were either the products of the imagination of the writers or actual accounts of the ministry of Jesus Christ. Norton could not believe that the Gospel writers possessed sufficient genius to have created the story of Jesus out of whole cloth or to have so embellished an ordinary life as to create a person of the stature of Jesus. He concluded that the consistency of the accounts, the simple manner of presentation, and the correlation between the Gospels and the history of the time were decisive proofs for their genuineness.[37] Furthermore, the presentation of Jesus was so striking and his system of religion so perfect that it was incredible that four anonymous and simple authors could have invented the whole.[38]

The effect of Norton's work on the genuineness of the Gospel was to substantiate the kind of authority he sought for his own religious faith. Since the Gospels were indubitably genuine, Jesus could be accepted as a divine messenger who had taught the perfect system of religion. On his authority the two foundations of all religion could be accepted: the existence of God and the immortality of man.[39]

[35] See, for example, the importance of the "change of scene" theory in Joachim Jeremias, *The Parables of Jesus*, S. H. Hooke, trans. (New York: Scribner's, 1955), pp. 23–30, 75–77.

[36] *Internal Evidences of the Genuineness of the Gospels* (Boston: Little Brown, 1855).

[37] *Internal Evidences*, pp. 219, 243, 244.

[38] *Internal Evidences*, pp. 245–47.

[39] *Genuineness*, II, lv–lvi.

[Jesus has] the character of a messenger from God, assuming in his name the highest authority, constantly exercising supernatural powers, and appearing among men for the purpose of making them acquainted with God, with their own immortal nature, with their duty, and with those ennobling and awful sanctions by which it is enforced. He is represented as discovering to men a perfect system of religion. He always appears, whether teaching, or acting, or suffering, as displaying the highest excellence. His character is everywhere consistent with itself and with the supernatural dignity of his office, though he is represented as passing through scenes the most trying and humiliating. We have, then, in these writings, a just conception of a perfect system of religion, as taught by a divine teacher, assuming the highest authority and exercising the most extraordinary powers, and displaying throughout a character in which we discover nothing but what is excellent and sublime.[40]

Like Locke, Norton accepted the miracles as proof of the divine authority of Jesus.[41] Clearly he believed that he had adequately defended Locke's principles. That which was essential to the Christian religion could be found in the Gospels, in a thoroughly credible narrative that was invulnerable to the attacks of later critics.

Norton's canon of the New Testament included the four Gospels, thirteen Epistles of Paul, and the first Epistles of John and Peter. He rejected other books, traditionally accepted as canonical, because they were anonymous or pseudonymous.[42] Within his canon, Norton gave primary importance to the Gospels.

[40] *Internal Evidences*, pp. 245–46.

[41] *Internal Evidences*, pp. 238–39. Norton regarded those who denied the reality of the miracles, even though they might accept true notions of Christian truth, as heretics. After Emerson's Divinity School address of 1838, Norton entered a lengthy debate with Emerson and George Ripley, defending the historicity of the miracles against "the latest form of infidelity." For an account of the miracles controversy, see William R. Hutchinson, *The Transcendentalist Ministers* (New Haven: Yale University Press, 1959), pp. 52–97.

[42] When Moses Stuart published his *A Commentary on the Epistle to the Hebrews* (2 vols.; Andover: Flagg and Gould, 1827, 1828), Norton responded with a series of articles disputing Stuart's contention that Paul had written the letter. See Norton, "On the Author of the Epistle to the Hebrews," *Christian Examiner,* IV (1827), 495–519; V (1828), 37–70; VI (1829), 198–225, 330–47.

There are certain books of the highest value, as constituting by far the most important documents from which we derive our knowledge of Christ and Christianity. These are, in the first place the historical books of the New Testament [the Gospels]; and in the next place the Epistles of St Paul and the other apostles. In the case of those apostles who were the immediate followers of our Lord, we thus distinguish their epistles from other books; because they give their testimony to the truth of his religion as eyewitnesses of his miracles, their minds had been formed by his instructions and the influence of his example, they had learnt the religion from him, and were commissioned by him to teach it. As regards St Paul, we believe him to have been miraculously called by Christ to be a preacher of Christianity; and concerning both him and the other apostles, we believe that their minds were enlarged and elevated by immediate communications from God, so that they were enabled to attain a correct comprehension of the character of the new dispensation.[43]

Norton did not regard as a revelation even the books that could be accepted into his canon. "[Revelation] . . . consists of a very few all important truths, the knowledge of which, if it had so pleased God, might have been preserved in books very different from those we now possess. . . ."[44] God had made his revelation in Jesus Christ, who had proclaimed those few authoritative truths. The New Testament merely preserved those truths so that they might become the foundation and standard for pure religion.[45] The genuineness of the books within Norton's canon guaranteed that the truths Jesus taught had been preserved for men of the nineteenth century.

Because Norton had no doubts about the validity of his standard of religious authority, he could adopt very critical positions at some points. He could even point to various passages that he considered spurious within the Gospels.[46] But to those who might be led to go

43 "Hebrews," pp. 343–44.

44 "Hebrews," p. 344.

45 "Hebrews," pp. 344–45.

46 Like many of his contemporaries, Norton thought the Gospel of Matthew to have been originally written in Hebrew and later translated into Greek. The whole of the first two chapters he thought to be an insertion of another text by the translator. *Genuineness,* I, 21 ff. In the same volume of this work, Norton included a long list of passages within the Gospels which he considered spurious (pp. liii–xc).

further Norton pointed out that he had spent a lifetime studying the subject, and warned them that there were no other spurious passages to be found. He had ascertained that nothing essential to Christian faith was in any way threatened by proper critical opinions.[47]

Norton had little interest in the critical study of the Old Testament. But in the second volume of his *Genuineness of the Gospels* he wrote an extended appendix on the relation of the Old Testament to the Christian faith.[48] When the Catholic church defended itself against the attacks of the Gnostics, Norton thought, it had committed a basic error in defending the Old Testament as a revelation from God. "Christianity has not made itself responsible for the genuineness, the authenticity, or the moral and religious teachings, of that collection of books by Jewish writers. . . ."[49] The Jews were guided by the providence of God, and their conception of religion was far superior to that of other ancient nations. But their canon contained much irrelevant and contradictory material, which had nothing to do with the revelation of God. God's revelation to the Jews was imbedded in myth, worthless liturgy, and inauthentic history. Because Norton believed Moses to have been a messenger from God, he could not believe that he was responsible for the writing of the Pentateuch, for so much of the Pentateuch contradicted the authoritative religious truths disclosed in the teaching of Jesus.

Norton feared that the critical attitude toward the Bible which had marked the American liberal party might lead to a thoroughgoing scepticism as it had in Germany. He attempted to arrest the progress of critical opinion in America by firmly establishing a bastion of truth which would be critical but conservative. He never doubted his own ability to discover the authoritative truths of Christianity and could little tolerate anyone who denied the propriety of consulting his educated opinion on the subject of liberal Christianity. Through his efforts he attempted to stabilize and consolidate the forces of American religious liberalism.

[47] *Genuineness,* I, lxix–lxx.
[48] *Genuineness,* II, xlviii–cc.
[49] *Genuineness,* II, xlviii.

CHAPTER VI

ARMING THE ORTHODOX

Moses Stuart: 1820–1852

No one was more convinced of the importance of Norton's work on the genuineness of the Gospels than Andover's Moses Stuart. After the first volume of *The Evidences of the Genuineness of the Gospels* appeared in 1837, Stuart wrote a seventy-eight page critical review for the *American Biblical Repository*,[1] hailing Norton's work as a great American scholarly achievement.

> Our country has hitherto been very sparing of contributions to the stock of sacred literature; at least of such as are the fruit of long and intense study, and the result of a widely extended knowledge of antiquities either sacred or profane. We have so few men who can afford to bury themselves for a long time in the closets of libraries, and so few libraries that have closets well stocked with books; withal we are so intent upon the *practical* business of life—on making our fortunes, or building up a mere temporary and popular fame, or grasping at office that we grow impatient under protracted years of effort in the acquisition of individual knowledge, and seldom endeavour to accomplish what the riper scholars of Europe are every day labouring to accomplish.[2]

Perhaps he had his old friend Everett in mind when he spoke of those who grasped for office rather than pursuing scholarly accomplishment.

Stuart welcomed Norton as an ally in the battle against radical criticism. In his years of teaching and writing at Andover he had

[1] XI (1838), 265–343.
[2] "Norton Review," p. 265.

attempted to anticipate all the objections that might be lodged against the system of evangelical orthodoxy he so warmly espoused. Well aware that German scholars were in the vanguard of biblical research, he eagerly read every new German contribution. He was shocked by the learned scepticism of the "neologists," a term of disapprobation applied to almost every non-orthodox German scholar. Nevertheless, he thought it quite possible to refute the neologists by careful, but reverential, research. Although neology had yet to make American converts, Stuart thought the day would soon come when the radical opinions of German scholars would be accepted by some Americans.

> Widely diffused as German literature is beginning to be in this country and in England, it is unwise, indeed it is impossible, for us to remain idle spectators of the great contest which has been and still is going on. If those who believe in and wish to defend either the genuineness, or the authenticity, or both, of the Old Testament and the New, choose to slumber on their post, and let neological views have their course without any effort to check or regulate them, they may be assured that in the end this country will see a revolution not unlike, in many respects, to that of Germany. There is no small part of our community, after all that we say and may justly say about the prevalence of Christian faith among us, who would be glad of an opportunity fairly to escape from the obligation which the Bible imposes upon their consciences.[3]

Norton's study received high praise from Stuart because in Stuart's mind Norton had thoroughly refuted the neological theories of Eichhorn, Gabler, and Paulus.

Stuart, of course, did not entirely agree with Norton's conclusions. Norton had been too free in admitting interpolations within the Gospels.[4] Because Stuart did not accept a Hebrew original of Matthew, and because he thought the style of Matthew to be consistent throughout, he particularly objected to Norton's classification of the first two chapters of that Gospel as interpolation.[5] He agreed

---

[3] "Norton Review," pp. 268-69.
[4] "Norton Review," p. 275.
[5] "Norton Review," p. 285.

with Norton that Mark and Luke were not intended as chrono-logical presentations of the life of Jesus, but argued that even Mat-thew had introduced chronology incidentally, because he had been witness to the events.[6]

Stuart's major disagreement with Norton concerned what he conceived to be an error of omission: Norton apparently did not accept the doctrine of biblical inspiration.[7] Norton had substanti-ated the credibility of the Gospels on intellectual grounds, and while the substance of Norton's faith might be perfectly acceptable be-cause it had been informed by the truths of the Scriptures, the mass of men could not be led to adequate Christian faith on this basis since they did not possess Norton's intellect.

> Any mere conviction of the genuineness of the gospels—any mere in-tellectual admission that they are correct and credible accounts of the life and doctrines of the Saviour—can and will never move the mass of men to yield to their *authority*. Does not Mr. Norton see, that this last point is so necessary, that all the rest being gained, nothing im-portant is gained unless this follow as a sequent to the others? But taking men as they are, with all that worldly spirit and all those de-sires of carnal indulgence which they possess and which they are for the most part heartily set upon gratifying, is there (humanly speak-ing) any chance to make real practical converts to Christianity, when the Scriptures are divested of *divine* authority, and made to extend no further than fallible human authority will go? [8]

Stuart was convinced that Norton's use of purely rational argu-ments to substantiate the authority of the Bible would ultimately lead others to scepticism.

Stuart's review of the *Genuineness of the Gospels* reveals his characteristic concerns as a biblical scholar and an orthodox evan-gelical. He was determined to erect an orthodox but rigorously crit-ical biblical science. Fearful of German neology he cautioned his colleagues to

6 "Norton Review," pp. 337–38.
7 "Norton Review," p. 340.
8 "Norton Review," p. 242.

prepare for the worst, . . . to take the vantage ground if we can in the contest, by shewing those who would attack the cause of settled belief in the Scriptures, that neither their attacks are unprovided for by us, nor their weapons or tactics unknown to us.[9]

Stuart's efforts to master German critical studies and use them in the cause of orthodoxy were never fully accepted by his conservative friends. Supporters of Andover Seminary continued to be concerned about the introduction to German opinion that students received in his classes. In 1825 the trustees of the Seminary appointed a special committee to investigate the problem. The committee reported that

the unrestrained cultivation of German studies has evidently tended to chill the ardor of piety, to impair belief in the fundamentals of revealed religion, and even to induce, for the time, an approach to universal skepticism.[10]

The committee further noted that while German studies might yield a greater knowledge of the Bible, Andover professors should urge their students to study the Bible with "reverence, meekness, simplicity, and implicit submission. . . ."[11] Not satisfied with a mere knowledge of the Bible, the investigators asked whether the new biblical studies had "brought forth any truth essential to salvation, or powerfully conducive to holiness?"[11]

The investigating committee need not have worried about Stuart's own reverence for the Bible. Throughout his Andover career his firm belief in the doctrine of scriptural inspiration preceded and directed all his critical studies.[12] But, unlike many conservatives, Stuart did not defend a doctrine of verbal inspiration of the

[9] "Norton Review," p. 270.
[10] Quoted by Daniel D. Williams in *The Andover Liberals* (New York: King's Crown Press, 1941), p. 17.
[11] Williams, *Andover Liberals,* p. 17.
[12] Williams states: "Not until the end of his life did [Stuart] express a definite conviction of divine inspiration for the entire Bible" (*Andover Liberals,* p. 17). This statement does not seem to accord with the evidence. In none of his publications or lectures does Stuart indicate any doubt of this doctrine.

Bible. His knowledge of the biblical texts made it impossible for him to believe that God had dictated the text of Scripture, for the original text had obviously been amended and corrupted in many instances, and God could not have allowed a corruption of his essential revelation. In regard to language, the Bible was like any other ancient book: *"When God has spoken to men, he has spoken in the language of men, for he has spoken by men, and for men."* [13] The scholar must understand the science of biblical languages and the history of biblical times in order to recover the meaning of biblical texts. In this regard he resembles the student of any other ancient literature. However, once the sense of a biblical passage has been discovered, the scholar has recovered God's inspired truth, for *unlike* any other ancient book, the subject matter of the Bible is the authoritative revelation of God.

Stuart's many publications reflected positions he had earlier espoused in the classroom. Since he thought that the subject matter of the Bible was the inspired revelation of God, Stuart could not believe that the Bible contained any real contradictions. God could not contradict himself. Because God was ultimately the author of Scripture, difficult and obscure passages in one portion might be explained by referring to a clear statement in another portion. This Stuart called "Scriptural analogy." [14]

Stuart maintained that the Bible contained one theology, for it had proceeded from one divine author. When he turned his attention to theological articles, he thought he was merely explicating

[13] *Elements of Interpretation, Translated from the Latin of J. A. Ernesti, and Accompanied by Notes and an Appendix Containing Extracts from Morus, Beck and Keil* (Andover: Mark Newman, 1827), p. 16. The quotation is from Stuart's addition to the translation, indicated in smaller type.

[14] "By Scriptural analogy I mean, that the obvious and incontrovertible sense of clear passages of Scripture affords a rule, by which we may reason analogically concerning the meaning of obscure passages; or at least, by which we may shew what obscure passages cannot mean. E.g. God is a spirit, is omniscient, supreme, the creator and governor of all things &c., are truths so plainly and incontrovertibly taught in the Scriptures, that all the passages which would seem to represent him as material, local [*sic*] limited in his knowledge or power &c. are to be interpreted agreeably to analogy with the former truths." *Ernesti,* pp. 17, 18.

this biblical theology. In an article for the *American Biblical Repository* entitled "Have the Sacred Writers Anywhere Asserted That the Sin or Righteousness of One is Imputed to Another?" Stuart indicated that the only source of Christian dogma was the Bible, "the unerring declarations of heaven." All other theology was church history, arguments, symbols, and decisions of "fallible and uninspired" men.[15] Stuart admitted that extra-biblical theological language might be "convenient on scientifical and didactical ground" and that systematic theology and technical expression might present and preserve the truths of Christian faith in a post-biblical age, but he maintained that only the theology of the Bible could be binding on any Christian.[16] For this reason he could see but a very limited use of creeds.

> Such are my views of creeds. Let a *biblical* use of them be made; let them be confined to fundamental doctrines; let mere manner of expression that is simply theological or technical, be not insisted on or made essential; let *things* and not words be the object; and with all my heart I agree to a creed. Beyond this, let all men beware how they entangle themselves. How can they, above all, bind themselves in the adoption of the sentiment, that the Scriptures are the *sufficient* and *only* rule of faith and practice, and yet profess to adopt a creed which inculcates what is extra-scriptural, or substitute mere manner of expression for matter of doctrine? Above all, let Protestants beware how they speak of any other *standard* than that of God's holy word.[17]

Stuart's view of theology and creeds stands midway between the position of Andover's founders and the position articulated by Horace Bushnell. Stuart was convinced that the exegesis of Scripture required that it be understood in its original sense, a conviction that saved him from proof-text theology. He strongly criticized the zealous orthodox who attempted to substantiate their doctrines with verses of Scripture taken out of their context and removed from the intent of the original author. Because he was so concerned with recovering the original meaning of the Scriptures, he devoted

[15] *American Biblical Repository,* VII (1836), 247.
[16] "Sacred Writers," p. 322.
[17] "Sacred Writers," p. 327.

a great deal of his energy to the production of commentaries on various biblical books.[18] Stuart's commentaries demonstrated his grasp of philological and grammatical tools of research. Although his conclusions always favored his conservative position, the commentaries represented a major advance over previous commentaries in the English language. He outlined guiding principles for the commentator on scriptural books in an article, "Hints Respecting Commentaries upon the Scriptures." [19] Here he maintained that the well-trained commentator should possess those philological and grammatical tools essential to the study of Scriptures in the original languages, for these tools were needed for the recovery of the original meanings of particular texts. But the commentator must also demonstrate an ability to penetrate the spirit of the author and to indicate the importance of the message contained in his writing. This could be accomplished best by the exegete who thoroughly accepted the inspiration of the Bible, for he could most readily illustrate the importance of a particular passage in light of the overarching unity of biblical theology. The capable commentator should not dwell too long on obscure and difficult passages. Such passages could ordinarily be explained in terms of the clear teaching of some other portion of the Bible, and if this were to fail, the commentator should confess that the passage "is beyond . . . [his] present ability to construe." [20]

Stuart sincerely admired the grammatical and philological scholarship of the Germans, and his own commentaries reflected his thorough acquaintance with their works. But he felt that German commentators rarely penetrated to the great truths the biblical authors presented.[21] This deficiency of German commentaries was compounded by the German proclivity for seeking contradictions, discrepancies, and problems within the biblical writings. For example, the Germans assumed as a matter of course that Peter and Paul would present different viewpoints, without considering that

18 For a list of Stuart's *Commentaries*, see the Bibliography.
19 *American Biblical Repository*, III (1833), 130–85.
20 "Hints Respecting Commentaries," pp. 140–41.
21 "Hints Respecting Commentaries," p. 146.

they were both authors of Scripture inspired by God and followers of the great teacher Jesus Christ.[22] Stuart, on the contrary, commended the "cautious and modest inquirer" who, when presented with an apparent problem, located the difficulty in his own inadequacy rather than in the inspired Bible.[23] In his lifetime as a biblical scholar Stuart had encountered many problems that seemed insoluble at the time but were later reconciled adequately to the whole of Christian truth. Basically, the great truths of Scripture were so plainly expressed that even the intelligent layman should have no difficulty in apprehending them. Stuart's success as a biblical critic was undoubtedly limited by this refusal to regard biblical problems as real rather than as merely apparent.

Stuart insisted on the absolute validity of biblical statements that had received sound grammatical and philological exegesis. This insistence led to an interesting interchange between the Andover professor and Professor Edward Hitchcock of Amherst concerning Genesis and geology.[24] Hitchcock was no German sceptic, but an evangelical American scientist interested in geology and concerned to maintain the validity of the Bible in the face of geological discoveries. In order to defend the Mosaic account of creation and to accommodate the geological evidence of the age of the earth before the appearance of organic life, he proposed a long span of time between the first and second days of creation. He accepted the creation story of Genesis with no question, but maintained that modern scientific discoveries afforded the interpreter of Scripture a new tool for understanding what Moses really meant to say.[25]

Stuart would have none of this.

[22] "Hints Respecting Commentaries," pp. 141–42.

[23] "Hints Respecting Commentaries," pp. 140–41.

[24] For this controversy, see Edward Hitchcock, "On the Connection between Geology and Natural Religion," *American Biblical Repository*, VI (1835), 113–137; Moses Stuart, "Critical Examination of Some Passages in Genesis i; with Remarks on Difficulties That Attend Some of the Present Modes of Geological Reasoning," *American Biblical Repository*, VII (1836), 46–106; and Edward Hitchcock, "Remarks on Professor Stuart's Examination of Gen. I. in Reference to Geology," *American Biblical Repository*, VII (1836), 448–86.

[25] Hitchcock, "Geology and Natural Religion."

I am unable to see how the discoveries of modern science and of recent date, can determine the meaning of Moses' words. Nothing can be more certain, than that the sacred writers did not compose their books with modern sciences in view, or indeed with any distinct knowledge of them. My own belief most fully is, that there is indeed nothing in the sacred books, which, when rightly viewed and interpreted according to the established principles of sound hermeneutics, will contradict any of the real and established maxims or principles of recent science.[26]

Stuart asserted that the biblical authors did not intend to teach the physical sciences and that therefore physical scientists could contribute nothing new to the art of exegesis. The plain teaching of Genesis indicated that the world had been created in six days. Geologists must decide whether they thought Moses, writing under the inspiration of God, was right or wrong. God's revelation in nature could not contradict his revelation in Scripture. For his part, he could not regard the science of geology sufficiently mature to challenge the authority of Scripture.[27]

Stuart published his major biblical work, *A Critical History and Defence of the Old Testament Canon,* in 1845.[28] He was nearing the end of his career, and his development of the arguments represents his mature thought. The book very nearly represented a critical introduction to the Old Testament, although Stuart, doubtless recalling the model of Eichhorn, disclaimed any intention of producing such a complete study. The volume was in part a response to Theodore Parker's American edition of De Wette's Old Testament *Introduction,*[29] but the argument was directed particularly at Andrews Norton, who, in the second volume of his *Genuineness of the Gospels,* had maintained that the Christian Church should not accept the authority of the Old Testament or make itself responsible for its contents. Stuart's volume reflected many of the

[26] "Geological Reasoning," p. 49.

[27] For a general discussion of this issue, see Conrad Wright, "The Religion of Geology," *New England Quarterly,* XIV (1941), 335–58.

[28] Andover: Allen, Morrill, and Wardwell, 1845.

[29] *A Critical and Historical Introduction to the Canonical Scriptures of the Old Testament from the German of Wilhelm Martin Leberecht De Wette* (2nd ed.; 2 vols.; Boston: Little, Brown, 1850).

positions he had taken in his class lectures on the Old Testament, and in general it is evident that his approach to the Bible had changed but little since he began his teaching career.

The basic argument of Stuart's *Defence* was straightforward and simple. The canon of Jewish Scripture had been completed before the advent of Christ. Jesus recognized the divine authority of the Jewish Scriptures. Anyone who accepted the authority of Jesus must accept the authority of the Old Testament.

Stuart argued that the Old Testament originated with the writings of Moses, on the ground that the leader of a nation in the long trek from Egypt to Palestine would of necessity have provided the community with laws, rules, and regulations. From time to time God had commanded Moses to institute and record particular legislation. Because Moses wrote when the occasion demanded or permitted, the style of the Pentateuch was uneven, and the subject matter often repetitious.

> To me the Pentateuch from the commencement of Moses' active public life onwards through the whole, wears the air of a (historical) *journal,* as well as a record of legislation which was engaged in as often as circumstances called for it. Everything is more or less minutely recorded, according to its relative importance at the time when it was written down. It looks exactly like the journal of a man, who was often interrupted in writing by the pressure of his other engagements. If Moses was actually the responsible leader of two and a half millions of people for forty years, through the Arabian desert, he most assuredly must have been a very busy man, and have had but little time for writing.[30]

The instructions for building the tabernacle illustrated the contemporaneity of Moses' writing: the detailed plans could hardly have been transmitted orally, and what would motivate a later writer to fabricate such an account?

In writing Genesis, Stuart maintained, Moses either combined traditions received from the Patriarchs or received a direct revelation from God concerning past historical events. In either case the

[30] *Defence,* p. 53.

material was authentic, for it had been transmitted by an inspired writer.

> Genesis . . . must have been matter of immediate revelation to Moses, or else of tradition either oral or written. It was for [Moses] to judge, as the traditions were examined by him what among them was true, and what was false. If we suppose him to have been under divine influence, (as I do suppose), the difficulty as to his judging would surely not be very great. The accounts of former times, then, he has brought together. I have no hesitation in believing that he has combined different ones; and occasionally, where the subject was one of deep interest, he extracted from two or more sources at the same time . . . .[31]

Stuart did not believe it mattered *who* wrote the works, or *when* they were written. They had, he believed, passed through Moses' hands and thus were authenticated by him. Of Deuteronomy's repetitions, he wrote:

> That a book of such claims as it puts forth, viz., as being a work of Moses the great lawgiver, should be composed at six different periods, as Ewald supposes, or at three or four, as Lengerke maintains, and yet admitted each time, by the whole Jewish nation, by prophets, priests, and kings, *as a genuine work of Moses,* requires much more credulity than the commonly received scheme of belief.[32]

Stuart thought that external testimony established the Mosaic authorship of the Pentateuch beyond question. No Jewish tradition was stronger than that of the Mosaic authorship, and Jesus himself had recognized Moses as the author of the first five biblical books.[33]

Stuart placed the next accession to the canon of the Old Testament during the reign of David and Solomon. This probably included extant portions of Joshua and Judges, two books he regarded as compilations dating from different historical periods.[34]

---

[31] *Defence*, pp. 54–55.

[32] *Defence*, pp. 54–55. Stuart's remarks concerning Deuteronomy were also particularly directed against the opinion of De Wette, who had identified Deuteronomy with the book discovered by Josiah in 621 B.C.

[33] *Defence*, p. 55.

[34] *Defence*, p. 97.

During the Davidic era the Hebrews began collecting the Psalms, most of which were written by David and his contemporaries, although the Psalter included some later amplifications.[35]

Stuart theorized that the temple, the religious center of Judaism, became the depository for canonical books. The prophets, who were charged with the duty of maintaining the purity of the Mosaic religion and were consulted on all important matters of religion and politics, guarded the canon.[36] No book could be added to the sacred collection without prophetic approval. Prophets were the inspired messengers of God, and their acceptance of a book authenticated its contents as surely as if it had been written by a prophet. Naturally, as soon as the succession of prophets ceased, the canon of the Old Testament was closed.[37]

Stuart relied heavily on the testimony of Josephus concerning the sacred Hebrew literature. Josephus, speaking for his countrymen, described how the succession of prophets had failed after the reign of Artaxerxes. Josephus regarded only those books composed by prophets or those of prophetic spirit as canonical.[38] The discrepancy between Josephus' list of twenty-two books and the thirty-nine found in the Old Testament Stuart reconciled by appealing to the Jewish custom of combining some books and considering them as one. Josephus' quotations from Scripture accounted for every Old Testament book except Job, which is used by Ezekiel and Philo of Alexandria. Stuart substantiated the evidence from Josephus by citing Philo and Jesus ben Sirach, whom he thought qualified to testify to Jewish practice, since both were priests or descendants of priestly families.[38]

The fact that the Jews were divided into Pharisaic and Sadducean parties in the time of Jesus further indicated that the canon had been closed by the days of Jesus' ministry. Neither party would allow the other to introduce a new book into the canon. "No one

[35] *Defence,* pp. 137–38.
[36] In this opinion Stuart followed many German critics, notably Bertholdt. See Parker, *Introduction from De Wette,* I, 33–36. Neither De Wette nor Parker accepted the theory.
[37] *Defence,* p. 231.
[38] *Defence,* pp. 312–13.

but a prophet divinely commissioned, and so endowed as to be acknowledged by both parties, would or could be entrusted with the introduction of a new sacred book." [39]

Therefore, Stuart concluded that in the days of Jesus the canon of the Old Testament had been closed. The last writing admitted to the canon was from the hand of Malachi, the last Jewish prophet in the line of succession. The Jewish people recognized a tripartite division of the canon: the Law, the Prophets, and the Writings.

Stuart had described the history of Old Testament Scripture within Judaism. He could now advance his crucial argument for the recognition of the Old Testament within Christianity.

> The Saviour says (Luke 24:44) to his doubting disciples: "All things must be fulfilled concerning me, which are written in the *Law of Moses* and the *Prophets,* and the *Psalms*." Now here is a distinct recognition of the threefold division of the Hebrew Scriptures, which is so expressly recognized in Sirach, by Philo, and by Josephus. It is impossible to entertain any reasonable doubt of this, considering the time and circumstances in which the words were uttered. And as we have already seen what books were included in this division, we of course must regard this as an appeal to the Jewish Canon, such as it now is. [40]

A few pages later Stuart sharpened the point of his argument.

> Christ was either in the right or in the wrong . . . . If he was in the right, then is the Old Testament a book of divine authority—the ancient revelation of God. If he was in the wrong, then we can put no confidence in his teaching. He might be in the wrong, with respect to every command and opinion which he gave; and of consequence the whole system of Christianity is nothing more than an airy figure moving in the *mirage,* or one which floats along upon the splendid mists which surround it. [41]

Stuart attempted to anticipate the arguments that might be used against his assertion. He rejected any idea that Jesus might merely have accommodated his teaching to the prevalent belief of the Jews.

[39] *Defence,* p. 295. Stuart had taken this argument from Eichhorn. See Parker, *Introduction from De Wette,* I, 43–45.
[40] *Defence,* p. 319.
[41] *Defence,* pp. 345–46.

To suppose him to have said this merely in the way of *accommodation* to Jewish prejudices about the meaning of the Old Testament, is neither more nor less than to suppose him guilty of fraud. If we should call it *pious fraud,* this would not better the case . . . . Or, as the only alternative, they must suppose the Saviour, like the Jews in general, to have either trifled with the meaning of the Scriptures, or to have been really ignorant of their true import. The responsibility of either of any of these assertions or suppositions, is what I would not desire to incur; and above all at the time when he, who is thus virtually accused of fraud or ignorance, shall sit as my Judge, in a trial whose results are to last for eternity.[42]

Nor could one deny that Luke had correctly reported the words of Jesus, for the New Testament was consistent in its testimony. One must either reject the whole of the New Testament or confess that he can "believe only such parts and so much of it, as . . . [he] may *a priori* judge to be probable and credible." [43]

Stuart's method of validating the Old Testament canon completely by-passed critical problems within the Old Testament. The authority of the Old Testament in no way depended upon the authorship, the manner, or the date of composition of Old Testament books. The Old Testament was the inspired word of God because it had either been written or approved by the prophets, whom God had inspired. The Old Testament was authoritative for the Christian Church because it had been endorsed by Jesus and his Apostles.[44]

In spite of the fact that Stuart thought he had established the inspiration and authority of the Old Testament beyond all question, from time to time he felt constrained to discuss particular critical problems. His study of Joshua and Judges had led him to conclude that they were both compilations of a number of documents.[45] He could not believe that Solomon wrote Ecclesiastes, because its style differed so radically from that of Proverbs.[46] Only sceptics could

[42] *Defence,* pp. 110–11.

[43] *Defence,* p. 320. Stuart thought Norton's study of the Old Testament was directed by this assumption.

[44] *Defence,* pp. 98–99.

[45] *Defence,* pp. 69, 152, 153.

[46] *Defence,* p. 139. He still regarded as binding the content of the book; see Stuart, *A Commentary on Ecclesiastes* (New York: Putnam, 1851).

doubt the history related in Jonah, because Christ had believed it, and God was capable of performing any miracle he pleased.[47] Stylistic differences within Isaiah convinced him that the book might have been written by two different authors, although because the prophets would not have perpetuated a fraud, the two authors probably had the same name: he suggested that the author of the second portion of the book be called "deutero-Isaiah" rather than "pseudo-Isaiah."[48] The books of Chronicles were particularly troublesome because they paralleled much of the material found in Kings, yet disagreed widely in detail. Stuart thought most of these problems arose from a corrupt text of Chronicles, particularly concerning numbers and dates.[49]

Stuart had no fear of examining the critical problems of the Old Testament. Since the Bible was the word of God it demanded examination.[50] The scholarly world would have no respect for the orthodox if they failed to recognize the critical problems within the Scriptures. Furthermore, without a due recognition of the problems involved, the orthodox might take indefensible positions. They had better be apprized of the facts so that they could adequately defend the Bible against all critics.[51]

Stuart did not presuppose the results of critical study, but he did presuppose the significance of critical results. All true conclusions about the problems of the Old Testament would point to its inspiration and authority, for those two facts had been guaranteed by Jesus and the prophets. In his lifetime of biblical study Stuart had seen many such problems resolved and felt assured that problems that still goaded his study would be resolved in the same way.[52]

Having substantiated the authority of the Old Testament to his own satisfaction, Stuart found it necessary to explain in what ways

[47] "The authority of Christ . . . seems to bind me to admit the *facts* as they are stated in the narrative of Jonah." *Defence,* p. 119.

[48] Stuart's suggestion has been adopted by critical scholars since. *Defence,* pp. 110–11.

[49] *Defence,* pp. 162–77.

[50] *Defence,* p. 176.

[51] *Defence,* pp. 176–77.

[52] *Defence,* pp. 18, 177.

the Jewish Scriptures were binding upon the Christian Church. He reduced this problem to one question.

What is there in the Old Testament, which belongs to JUDAISM as such; and what is there which belongs to THE NATURE OF TRUE RELIGION, at all times, among all nations, and in all places?

That which belongs merely to Judaism as such, is wholly abolished by the Gospel. WHAT BELONGS TO ALL NATIONS IS FULLY RETAINED. The proper application of these two simple principles, is all that is necessary to a right understanding of this whole subject.[53]

In a sense Stuart's whole effort had been directed toward substantiating the theological claim that the Protestant Bible was the inspired word of God, rather than toward establishing the authority of the Old Testament. The Old Testament could claim only the authority allowed by the New Testament, for the latter was the "highest tribunal" in matters of religion.[54]

Stuart's *Defence* was vulnerable to several criticisms. Critics could demonstrate that the canon of the Old Testament had not been determined by the beginning of the first century: the books included in the Writings, the third division of the Hebrew Scriptures, were not determined until the beginning of the second century A.D. Josephus' statement concerning the failure of the Jewish prophetic tradition signified the initiation, rather than the termination, of the canonization of the Old Testament. Stuart's theory of a school of prophets who were connected with the temple and who passed approval on writings admitted to Jewish Scripture was totally unsubstantiated and overlooked the persistence of "false prophets" within Judaism. If the prophets guaranteed the authority of the writings, who guaranteed the authority of the prophets? By what standards were false prophets distinguished from the prophets sent from God? Finally, if the use of the Old Testament by the authors of the New testified to the divine authority of the former, other writings, quoted and paraphrased, should have authority equal to that of the Old Testament. On these grounds, Stuart would have

[53] *Defence,* p. 388.
[54] *Defence,* p. 417.

been logically compelled to accept the books of the Apocrypha and Pseudepigrapha into the canon of the Christian Scripture.

From his position at Andover Seminary, Stuart endeavored to foster the growth of an orthodox tradition of biblical scholarship in America. It is not surprising that his efforts met with little lasting success. Stuart felt an urgent need to defend orthodoxy against the liberals and neologists with biblical studies. But German neology failed in America not because of brilliant orthodox defense, but rather because of lack of interest; the great battle among American religious parties was waged in the pulpit rather than in the classroom. The mass of Americans were more readily led to accept the authority of the Bible by rhetoric than by logic. Time and again Stuart stated that the truths of the Bible were so explicit that any man of common sense could understand them and grasp the principles of interpretation which would authenticate them. Since the truths of the Bible were so obvious, it could easily seem a work of supererogation to master biblical languages and read extensively the arid productions of continental scholars. Finally, Stuart's repeated assurances that all the problems of the Bible could be reconciled with orthodox dogma made the problems seem unimportant; whatever solution might be finally determined, it would substantiate the divine authority of the Bible.

CHAPTER VII

THEIR FINEST HOUR

Edward Robinson and the Exploration of Palestine

Stuart's achievements at Andover were overshadowed by the accomplishments of his most famous pupil, Edward Robinson, the one American scholar to achieve an international reputation in biblical studies before the Civil War. Robinson was born in 1794, the son of a Connecticut Congregational minister. Because the family lacked the means to finance his education, he left home in 1812 to live with a paternal uncle who taught at Hamilton College. He graduated from Hamilton at the head of the class of 1816 and remained there, tutoring in Greek and Mathematics. In 1818 he married the sister of Harvard's President Kirkland, but unfortunately she died within the year. In 1821 Robinson moved to Andover to supervise the publication of his edition of a Greek text of the *Iliad*. While in Andover he enrolled in the Seminary and immediately became interested in Moses Stuart's biblical pursuits.[1]

In 1823 Robinson was appointed Instructor in Hebrew at the Seminary, a position he held until 1826. During these years he joined with Stuart's effort to publish useful texts, working with Stuart on the revision of his Hebrew grammar, on the translation and publication of Winer's *Grammar of the Greek New Testa-*

---

[1] For a sketch of Robinson's life, see Henry B. Smith and Roswell D. Hitchcock, *The Life, Writings and Character of Edward Robinson, D.D., LL.D.* (New York: Randolph, 1863); and William F. Albright, "Edward Robinson," in *Dictionary of American Biography* (New York: Scribner's, 1936), XVI, 39–40.

ment, and, unassisted, translating and publishing Wahl's *Clavis
Philologica Novi Testamenti.*[2]

In 1826, probably with Stuart's encouragement, Robinson resigned his position at the Seminary to continue his studies in Germany. Like Everett and Bancroft before him, Robinson went first
to Göttingen, but during the next four years he continued his studies
primarily at the universities at Halle and Berlin.

Robinson was both impressed and distressed by German theological education. He painfully acknowledged that German biblical
criticism had resulted in a rejection of the principle he had learned
from Stuart, namely, that "the Bible was *the only and sufficient
rule of faith and practice.*"[3] In this, Robinson thought, the German
critics betrayed the heritage of the Reformation. But, he hastened to
add, this irreverent criticism was already producing "a reaction,
which promises, by the blessing of God, in time to bring back the
German churches to the faith and practice of the Gospel. . . ."[4]
Robinson marvelled at the competence and training of German professors. In America men of prominence were sometimes given pro-
fessorships, and only subsequently were expected to master their
fields. In Germany, however, the universities were involved in a
constant process of training new professors from the ranks of those
receiving advanced degrees and occupying lesser ranks of instruction. Furthermore, the wealth of scholars made highly specialized
fields possible, so that "the system of a division of labour is here
carried to as high a point in regard to intellectual employment, as
it is in England in respect to manual occupations."[5] Of course,
Robinson was equally impressed by the breadth and originality of

[2] *A Greek Grammar of the New Testament: Translated by Moses Stuart
and Edward Robinson from the German of George Benedict Winer* (Andover:
Flagg and Gould, 1825); Edward Robinson, *A Greek and English Lexicon of
the New Testament from the "Clavis Philologica" of Abraham Wahl* (Andover: [Flagg and Gould?], 1825).

[3] Edward Robinson, "Theological Education in Germany," *The Biblical Repository,* I (1831), 1–51, 201–26, 409–51.

[4] "Theological Education," p. 3.

[5] "Theological Education," p. 49.

individual scholars, particularly, at Halle, the biblical scholar and Hebrew grammarian Gesenius and the theologian Tholuck; and, at Berlin, the church historian Neander, the theologian Schleiermacher, and the geographer Ritter.

Of all his teachers probably Gesenius and Ritter were most influential. Gesenius' critical methods of study in the Old Testament certainly seemed irreverent to Robinson, but this did not deter his great interest in that scholar's mastery of the Hebrew language.[6] Ritter apparently interested Robinson in geography and probably encouraged his inclination to combine the disciplines of geography and biblical research in a study of the geography of Palestine.

In 1828 Robinson married Therese Jacob, whose father was Professor of Philosophy and Political Science at Halle. Therese was a devoted wife, and Robinson's ties with Germany and German scholarship were strengthened by his marriage.

Robinson resumed his connection with Andover upon returning to America in 1830. For three years he served as Librarian and Professor Extraordinary of Sacred Literature. These must have been particularly pleasant years for Moses Stuart, for he was at last associated with a colleague trained in the German school of biblical research. Stuart hoped that some endowment might be given the Seminary to insure the position of his younger friend. But the desired funds did not materialize, and Robinson's health began to deteriorate from repeated attacks of epilepsy. Consequently, he resigned his position in 1833 and moved to Boston.

The years at Andover had been productive ones for Robinson. In 1832 he published his own edition of Calmet's *Dictionary of the Bible*. Calmet's *Dictionary* had been published in France in 1730 and, revised and translated, published in England in 1732. Robinson made considerable deletions of material he considered fanciful and below the standard of developing scholarship, particularly in the areas of philology, interpretation, and geography. He substituted new material drawn from recent German scholars; and he worked

[6] Seminarians of the twentieth century are still familiar with Gesenius' grammatical and lexicographical works.

particularly hard on the geographic and cartographic sections, employing accounts of recent travellers in biblical lands.[7] A year later Robinson published a more complete grammar for Greek, this one from the German Buttmann, because he had come to feel that Winer's grammar, which he and Stuart had published in 1825, had been superseded.[8]

A far more ambitious and potentially a far more important project was the initiation of a new scholarly journal, *The Biblical Repository,* whose first issue appeared in 1831 under Robinson's editorial supervision. Robinson envisioned a publication that would serve as a clearing house for all the most recent and important biblical scholarship both in Germany and in America. Undoubtedly he expected that those already involved in biblical studies would welcome the opportunity to write for the *Repository* and to acquaint themselves with the researches of others. In addition, such a periodical might well stimulate the growth of an American scholarly community interested in biblical research. However, at least in practice, the journal never transcended the lines of American denominationalism. The few who wrote for the *Repository* were drawn from a circle of those sympathetic to the Andover Seminary and its theological position.

Robinson worked prodigiously for the success of *The Biblical Repository.* During the four years he served as editor of the publication he wrote for its pages twenty original articles and translated twenty-seven more. His mentor, Moses Stuart, contributed fourteen articles, and Robinson's wife contributed two. Only thirty-eight articles by others were published. In spite of the commendation of many readers, interest in the critical study of the Bible in America had not grown sufficiently to support a scholarly journal, especially one that was also bounded by a set theological position. When Robinson resigned as editor in 1834, he acknowledged the toll of time

[7] *Calmet's Dictionary of the Holy Bible* (Boston: Crocker and Brewster; New York: Leavitt, 1832). The *Dictionary* was not copyrighted and went through numerous editions.

[8] Phillipp Karl Buttmann, *Buttmann's "Larger Greek Grammar": Translated from the German with Additions by Edward Robinson* (Andover: Flagg, Gould, and Newman; New York: Leavitt, 1833).

and labor the periodical had required of him, and under new editors the journal became a general religious publication.[9]

Robinson's articles and translations for *The Biblical Repository* afford a means of surveying his own interests during this period. He remained essentially conservative in his attitudes, at times even more conservative than his teacher, Moses Stuart. Among the translations he offered his American readers were excerpts from Hengstenberg's *Christologie des Alten Testaments*. Unlike Stuart, Robinson, following Hengstenberg, was convinced that Isaiah was the work of one author. With Hengstenberg he accepted the messianic interpretation of Isaiah, although he could not endorse Hengstenberg's mechanical conception of prophecy, namely that God had caused Old Testament prophets to utter truths of which they were unaware.[10] From time to time Robinson felt obligated to express his reservations about German scholarship. After all, Moses Stuart's inclinations for Germany had frequently been cause for alarm in the past. In an original article giving an exegesis of the Song of Deborah in Judges, chapter five, Robinson criticized his admired teacher Gesenius for supposing that the Song was older than the Book of Numbers because Numbers counted six hundred thousand soldiers in Israel while the Song mentions only forty thousand. Robinson accepted the Mosaic authorship of Numbers and the historical accuracy of the enumeration given there of Israel's forces; the enumeration in Judges he thought to be a poetic exaggeration.[11] Robinson's continuing interest in biblical geography can be seen in his article "Exodus of the Israelites out of Egypt, and Their Wanderings in the Desert." [12]

In an article written during the last year of his editorship,

[9] In 1843 Robinson again attempted to found a journal of biblical studies. For one year he served as editor of *Bibliotheca Sacra*. Although he maintained an association with the journal until 1857, the editorship shifted to Andover in 1844, and this journal, too, became a general religious periodical.

[10] "Genuineness of Isaiah, Chap. XL–LXVI, from Hengstenberg's *Christologie des Alten Testaments*," Robinson, ed., *The Biblical Repository*, I (1831), 700–33.

[11] "Song of Deborah and Barak," *The Biblical Repository*, I (1831), 568–612. Modern scholars follow Gesenius.

[12] *The Biblical Repository*, II (1832), 743–97.

Robinson found occasion to discuss the general state of biblical studies in America. He clearly recognized the derivative nature of American biblical scholarship: Europe possessed the biblical manuscripts; America had none. More important, Europe, and particularly Germany, possessed the traditions of scholarly research supported by a university system and employing vast numbers of learned men working on specialized subjects and problems. Until Americans could develop their own traditions, they must rely on the output of the continental scholars; even scholarship in England, in Robinson's opinion, did not yet compare with American efforts.[13] But Robinson did not expect American seminaries, colleges, and universities to establish such traditions; instead, although he recognized the difficulties of his expectations, he looked to the clergy to assume in America the role university professors had assumed in Germany.

> It is to the clergy, that we must principally look for the successful cultivation of this species of literature; and it is hardly necessary to remark, that the life of active and laborious exertion, to which most of them are called at the present day, is ill adapted to that extensive progress in any department, which is usually the result only of long and painful effort directed to a single point, and carried on in retirement from the bustle of the world, and without the pressure of those claims of active and public duty, which, in the case before us, are paramount to every other.[14]

Biblical scholarship among the clergy at this time had to compete for attention with a host of organized activities such as home and foreign missionary societies, revivals, and social reform organizations —the American Bible Society, the American Tract Society, and the American Temperance Society. Robinson sympathized with these

[13] Robinson's evaluation of English biblical studies was quite accurate. After the career of Herbert Marsh, British scholars seemed little involved with problems of the new criticism until the appearance of the famous *Essays and Reviews* of 1860 and the Bishop Colenso affair which followed shortly thereafter. See J. Estlin Carpenter, *The Bible in the Nineteenth Century* (London: Longmans, Green, and Co., 1903).

[14] "Philology and Lexicography of the New Testament," *The Biblical Repository*, IV (1834), 155–56.

activities and supported the clerical concern in them. However, because he expected the clergy to recognize that all of these activities depended on the Bible as "the sufficient and only rule of faith and practice," he also expected Americans to support the cultivation of biblical studies.

After Robinson resigned his positions at Andover and *The Biblical Repository,* he set about the task of preparing Gesenius' famous Hebrew lexicon for an American edition. He made few changes, for Gesenius' work was easily the best Hebrew lexicon available, quite possibly the best lexicon of any language published up to that time. The work was issued in 1836, and in subsequent years Robinson altered it according to later German editions.[15]

In 1837 Robinson accepted an appointment to the recently established Union Theological Seminary in New York. The trustees of the institution granted Robinson's request to delay the beginning of his duties for three or four years to permit his exploration and study in Palestine. Thus began those explorations and publications that would earn Robinson an international scholarly reputation and establish him as the foremost Palestinologist of his day.

Robinson and his wife sailed from New York in July, 1837. After brief visits in England and Germany, where Robinson renewed acquaintances with Gesenius and others and where he apparently left his wife with her family, Robinson travelled to Cairo. In Cairo he joined the Reverend Eli Smith, who was to be his companion traveller in Palestine. Smith had been a pupil of Robinson's at Andover, and after graduation had become a missionary stationed at Beirut. When Smith returned on furlough to Andover in 1832, his reports of his journeys intensified Robinson's desire to explore Palestine. Robinson's choice of Smith as a companion was particularly important because of the missionary's mastery of Arabic.

Robinson and Smith set out from Cairo in early March, 1838. Travelling by way of Suez, across the Sinai Peninsula, and along

---

[15] Friedrich Heinrich Wilhelm Gesenius, *A Hebrew and English Lexicon of the Old Testament, Including the Biblical Chaldee: Translated from the Latin of William Gesenius by Edward Robinson* (Boston: Crocker and Brewster; New York: Leavitt, Lord, & Co., 1833).

the shores of the Gulf of Aqaba, they entered Palestine in early April, and by the end of June had reached Beirut and the end of their journey. Throughout their travels Robinson kept a meticulous daily journal, recording everything of possible historical, geographical, topographical, or personal interest. This daily journal formed the basis for his subsequent publication.

Following his journeys through the Middle East, Robinson returned to Berlin to complete a manuscript. He used the personal collections of his German colleagues and the Royal Library for comparisons with the accounts of others and completed the manuscript in 1840. His wife immediately translated the manuscript into German; galleys were sent from Boston to London before publication, and in 1841 the *Biblical Researches in Palestine* was published simultaneously in Halle, London, and Boston. Robinson dedicated the German edition to the geographer Ritter; the English edition was dedicated to Moses Stuart, as "the fruit of studies begun in the bosom of his family. . . ."

Robinson's *Researches* enjoyed immediate critical acclaim. Without doubt it was the most significant piece of American Biblical scholarship before the Civil War. More significant, Robinson's work laid the foundation for all subsequent geographical and archaeological study in Palestine. In recognition of the importance of his study, the Royal Geographical Society of London awarded him its gold medal in 1842.

The *Biblical Researches* was distinguished for its painstakingly critical historical judgments about traditional Palestinian geography. Robinson would not rely upon the accounts of previous travellers. Instead, he attempted to reconstruct the geography of ancient Palestine, in so far as that was possible, using only the Bible, the toponymic traditions of its contemporary inhabitants, and his own critical observations.

Robinson's criticism of traditional Palestinian geography was severe, at times almost scathing. Frequently in the *Biblical Researches* he found occasions to deride "monkish traditions." One extended example will serve to illustrate the rigor of this criticism.

I must request the reader to bear in mind, that for the lapse of more than fifteen centuries, Jerusalem has been the abode not only of mistaken piety, but also of credulous superstition, not unmingled with pious fraud. During the second and third centuries after the Christian era, the city remained under heathen sway; and the Christian church existed there, if at all, only by sufferance. But when, in the beginning of the fourth century, Christianity became triumphant in the person of Constantine; and at his instigation . . . the first great attempt was made in A.D. 326, to fix and beautify the places connected with the crucifixion and resurrection of the Saviour; it then, almost as a matter of course, became a passion among the multitudes of priests and monks, who afterwards resorted to the Holy City, to trace out and assign the site of every event, however trivial or legendary, which could be brought into connection with the Scriptures or with pious tradition. The fourth century appears to have been particularly fruitful in the fixing of these localities, and in the dressing out of the traditions or rather legends, which were attached to them. But the invention of succeedings ages continued to build upon these foundations, until, in the seventh century, the Muhammedan conquest and subsequent oppressions confined the attention of the church more exclusively to the circumstances of his present distress; and drew off in part the minds of the clergy and monks from the contemplation and embellishment of Scriptural history. Thus the fabric of tradition was left to become fixed and stationary as to its main points; in much the same condition, indeed, in which it has come down to our day. The more fervid zeal of the ages of the crusades, only filled out and completed the fabric in minor particulars.[16]

Robinson was careful in his own study to compare his conclusions with the accounts of as many travellers as possible. These he carefully footnoted. But for the most part he rejected these traditions, in many cases explicating the process of historical misinterpretation which had made them accepted. A modern Palestinologist makes this appraisal of Robinson's work:

[He] seems to have been the first to understand this [mistaken traditional topography], and he was certainly the first scholar who ana-

[16] *Biblical Researches in Palestine* (3 vols.; Boston: Crocker and Brewster, 874), I, 251–52. Citations are made from the 11th ed., which includes the account of Robinson's later explorations.

lyzed it with the methods of historical criticism, instead of treating it with unfruitful skepticism. We may justly suppose that this was the first decisive methodical advance which he made in his study of the literature. Without the critical use of sources, according to the methods which he first recognized as necessary, no scientific Palestinology was thenceforth possible; he himself worked along this line with so much energy and with such great success that he was able definitively to disprove a large part of what his predecessors had thought and written. In Robinson's footnotes are forever buried the errors of many generations.[17]

Robinson's discovery of local toponymic traditions, in which he was greatly assisted by his Arabic-speaking companion, led him to seek new sites off the beaten path of pious pilgrims. Still, his identifications were not made simply on the basis of phonetic similarity. He maintained his critical attitude and insisted on some topographic or historical substantiation before making positive identification. His reluctance to make positive identification without ample proof sometimes led him to make suggestions that later proved fruitful to archaeologists.[18]

Robinson's reverence and respect for the Bible grew in the course of his researches. He frankly informed his readers that his first motive in exploring Palestine had been the "gratification of personal feelings: which had been aroused from hearing and reading the Bible in pious New England." [19] Time and again Robinson was able to identify sites simply by referring to appropriate scriptural passages, and thus he came increasingly to accept the absolute accuracy of the Bible.

As a critical scholar Robinson could understand how erroneous traditions had grown in Palestine in post-biblical times. But because he was committed to Stuart's theological understanding of the Bible, he could not turn on the Bible itself the techniques he had so fruit-

[17] Albrecht Alt, "Edward Robinson and the Historical Geography of Palestine," *The Journal of Biblical Literature*, LVIII (1939), 374.

[18] See F. M. Abel, "Edward Robinson and the Identification of Biblical Sites," *The Journal of Biblical Literature*, LVIII (1939), 365–72.

[19] *Researches*, I, 31–32.

fully employed on the post-biblical period. Nor could he imagine that the biblical religious communities had fabricated religious traditions as the post-biblical communities had done. Robinson held firmly to the belief in the Mosaic authorship and the accuracy of the Pentateuch when he stood on the shores of the Red Sea at Suez selecting a spot he felt appropriate for the miraculous crossing by the fleeing Israelites. Robinson had no difficulty explaining how God could use a strong northeast wind at ebb tide to create a dry crossing, but the Book of Numbers led him to conclude that the Israelites numbered over two million persons, who, together with their flocks and herds, crossed the sea within the space of two hours.[20] Had this been a "monkish tradition" rather than a biblical one, Robinson would undoubtedly have grasped the enormity of supposing that two million fleeing and disorganized refugees could have been so quickly transported across the Red Sea. As a modern scholar points out, such a host marching in close order would have extended from Egypt to Sinai and back.[21] But even a problem of this magnitude could not bring him to exercise his critical powers on the Bible. Although he could not fully understand how the multitudes had crossed the sea, the Bible said it had happened: God did it.

Robinson's reverence for the Bible was further reinforced by the religious awe he felt while travelling through biblical lands and standing on biblical sites. Although he was certainly the most critical pilgrim yet to visit the Promised Land, he was a pilgrim nonetheless, and probably few pilgrims expressed more fervently their frank emotions. The *Researches* abound in references to his religious feelings when approaching hallowed scenes and in descriptions of the prayers, devotions, and scripture readings of his party. Describing the approach of the travellers to Sinai, Robinson wrote:

> I was affected by the strangeness and overpowering grandeur of the scenes around us; and it was for some time difficult to realize, that we were now actually within the very precincts of that Sinai, on which from the earliest childhood I had thought and read with so much

[20] *Researches*, I, 56–59.
[21] See John Bright, *A History of Israel* (Philadelphia: Westminster, 1959), p. 121.

wonder. Yet, when at length the impression came with its full force upon my mind, although not given to the melting mood, I could not refrain from bursting into tears.[22]

And again, when the small band first entered Palestine at Beersheba, Robinson could scarcely contain his exhilaration:

> Here then is the place where the patriarchs Abraham, Isaac, and Jacob often dwelt! Here Abraham dug perhaps this very well; and journeyed from hence with Isaac to Mount Moriah, to offer him up there in sacrifice. From this place Jacob fled to Padan-Aram, after acquiring the birthright and blessing belonging to his brother; and here too he sacrificed to the Lord on setting off to meet his son Joseph in Egypt. Here Samuel made his sons judges; and from here Elijah wandered out into the southern desert, and sat down under a shrub of Retem just as our Arabs sat down under it every day and every night. Here was the border of Palestine proper, which extended from Dan to Beersheba. Over these swelling hills the flocks of the patriarchs once roved by thousands; where now we found only a few camels, asses, and goats! [23]

The dedication of the German edition of the *Researches* to Ritter and the English edition to Stuart seems appropriate, for the volumes represent a curious combination of German critical scholarship and New England piety.

When he returned to New York in 1841 Robinson immediately resumed his labors in the field of biblical philology. Textual researches in Germany had proceeded so rapidly that Griesbach's New Testament text had been superseded. In 1842 he supervised the publication of Tittmann's *Novum Testamentum Graece*.[24] Ever the thorough scholar, Robinson worked to keep his grammatical and philological publications current with latest research. The New Testament grammar and text, the Hebrew lexicon, and other works were

[22] *Researches*, I, 91.

[23] *Researches*, I, 205.

[24] This text of the New Testament is not listed in either the printed catalogs of the Library of Congress or in the printed catalogs of the British Museum. However, see Julius A. Bewer, "Edward Robinson as a Biblical Scholar," *The Journal of Biblical Literature*, LVIII (1939), 356–57.

through several editions with Robinson making the necessary changes in each new edition.[25]

In 1852, again in the company of Eli Smith, Robinson returned to Palestine. At that time he was planning a complete geography of Palestine, and there were many questions and problems he thought could be resolved only by a visit to that country. From April to July he and Smith travelled over new routes, and Robinson made several new identifications. In method and procedure his journey resembled his earlier visit to Palestine. The third volume of the *Biblical Researches* appeared in 1856. By that time Robinson was busily engaged in the preparation of a complete biblical geography, but his health had been declining rapidly since 1856, and his work unfortunately was unfinished when he died in 1863.

In his system of hermeneutics Robinson committed himself thoroughly to the precepts of his teacher, Moses Stuart. In his inaugural address, "The Bible and Its Literature," delivered at the Union Theological Seminary in 1841, he surveyed those aspects of his discipline necessary to the biblical scholar.[26] As he spoke of the necessity of mastering the biblical languages, he pointed with pride to the remarkable production of grammars, lexicons, and critical texts by American scholars, noting that Americans had supplied these tools for their English colleagues. Robinson encouraged the would-be scholars in his audience to become familiar with that thorough knowledge encompassed by German scholars under the rubric of "Biblical Introduction," which included the knowledge of textual sources, versions, authors, dates, styles, geography, and historical chronology. The scholar must be adequately acquainted with the biblical text, and Robinson emphasized that no scholar could commit himself to a theory of inspiration that depended on an infallible text, for it could be readily seen that many variant readings and corruptions had been introduced during the transmission of these writings.[27] The basic hermeneutical principle that must guide the biblical scholar was the

---

[25] On this aspect of Robinson, see Bewer, "Robinson," pp. 355–63.

[26] *The Bible and Its Literature* (New York: Office of the *American Biblical Repository*, 1841).

[27] See "Philology and Lexicography of the New Testament," cited above.

explication of the text as it would have been understood by its original author and audience. On this point Robinson could not avoid an allusion to his travels:

> It was with an absorbing and exciting interest that we . . . visited these [biblical] spots; it was almost like communing with these holy men themselves; and served in a high degree, to give us a deeper impression of the reality and vividness of the Scriptural narrative, and to confirm our confidence in the truth and power of the sacred volume.[28]

And finally, while he granted that the department of systematic theology was responsible for developing the doctrine of inspiration, he reminded his audience:

> It has ever been the glory of the Protestant Faith, that it has placed the Scriptures where they ought to be, above every human name, above every human authority. THE BIBLE IS THE ONLY AND SUFFICIENT RULE OF FAITH AND PRACTICE.[29]

Within the principles Robinson learned from his mentor he had forged a career that placed him internationally within the first rank of biblical scholars. No other American before the Civil War accomplished so much. But despite Robinson's accomplishments, his hope for the creation of a community of biblical scholars was in vain. Neither the clergy nor the seminaries and colleges supported such studies adequately; and in 1863 Robinson died without a successor.

[28] *The Bible and Its Literature*, pp. 40–41.
[29] *The Bible and Its Literature*, p. 17.

CHAPTER VIII

A GENERAL WITHOUT TROOPS

George R. Noyes and the Decline of Liberal Biblical Studies

AFTER Channing's Baltimore sermon Andrews Norton had shifted the area of discussion from biblical interpretation to theological formulation, and since then there had been little public discussion between the several parties about biblical studies. Denominational lines also separated scholarly communities. Even Stuart's *Defence of the Canon of the Old Testament,* so obviously aimed against the Unitarians, did not draw the rebuttal which might have been expected. Andrews Norton, against whom Stuart directed much of his argument and to whom he had sent a copy of the book, made no public reply. Instead, he wrote to Stuart,

> If I had more health and leisure I might be tempted to make a few observations on your work, intended only for yourself. But, perhaps, it would in any case be scarcely worth while. At our period of life it cannot be expected, that either of us should essentially affect the others' opinions, and we are both drawing near to that state where all our errors will be corrected, and where it is my faith that no errors conscientiously entertained will be laid to our account.[1]

Norton had lost the reforming zeal that had originally motivated liberal scholars to a critical study of the Bible.

Stuart's *Defence* did not, however, pass without notice within the

---

[1] The Norton-Noyes correspondence, as well as the other Norton letter referred to in this chapter, is with the Norton Papers (MSS in the Houghton Library, Harvard University). In two cases letters are in Letter Book B; other letters are referred to by date only. The present letter is dated 20 September 1845, Letter Book B, p. 271.

Unitarian camp. In 1846 in a review for the *Christian Examiner*[2] and in the introduction to his *New Translation of the Proverbs, Ecclesiastes, and Canticles*,[3] George R. Noyes replied to Stuart. Noyes concurred with Stuart in dating the closing of the Old Testament canon before the days of Jesus.[4] But he could not agree that Jesus had given the weight of his authority to the Old Testament.[5] He maintained that Jesus came to establish the doctrines of Christianity, and that he referred to the Old Testament as did other Jews of the day. To be sure, Jesus indicated that much of the Old Testament contained divine revelation, but

> If Jesus Christ has settled by his divine authority all the various questions which have arisen in regard to the character, criticism, and meaning of the Old Testament, then one object of his coming into the world was to set bounds to criticism, the inevitable consequence of which would be to put a stop to that mental improvement and that exact knowledge which are the result of criticism. For it is idle to pretend that we have a right to study the Old Testament critically, unless we have a right to judge of its contents according to the laws of critical and historical investigation. I cannot believe that the design of Christ's coming into the world was to put a stop to any scientific investigation.[6]

Noyes buttressed his case by denying that the religious teaching of Jesus could be harmonized with the Old Testament. He who taught his disciples to pray for their enemies could scarcely have thought God would command the Israelites to exterminate the Canaanites. He who died praying for his enemies could scarcely have accepted the "horrible imprecations" of some of the Psalms.[7] Noyes felt that Stuart's book might induce many rational and moral men to forsake Christianity, because in it he had implied that those who rejected the authority and inspiration of the Old Testament should reject the authority of Jesus. Because Stuart had removed the question of Old

2 "Stuart on the Old Testament," XL (1846), 69–77.

3 Boston: James Munroe, 1846.

4 "Stuart," p. 69.

5 *Proverbs, Ecclesiastes, Canticles*, p. 139.

6 *Proverbs, Ecclesiastes, Canticles*, pp. 139–40.

7 *Proverbs, Ecclesiastes, Canticles*, pp. 138–40.

Testament authority from critical and historical investigation, many would forsake honest study of the Old Testament to preserve their Christian faith.

Noyes denied that any community, whether Jewish or Christian, had authority to make a particular book binding for his own faith and practice. The critical inquirer must consider each book separately, determine its own claims for religious authority, and weigh the internal and external claims in its support. The Canticles, for example, must be judged by aesthetic standards, as a piece of amatory poetry, not as authoritative revelation.[8]

George Rapall Noyes was the first thoroughly competent Old Testament scholar within the liberal movement and, in 1845, the only Unitarian who could match Stuart's mastery of Old Testament criticism. Noyes, born in 1798, graduated in the Harvard class of 1818 and was one of the first students to take advantage of the new Department of Divinity organized at Harvard in 1819. At Harvard Noyes apprenticed himself to Andrews Norton and remained in Cambridge until 1827, pursuing theological and biblical studies. From 1827 until 1840 he served the parishes of Brookfield and Petersham, Massachusetts, and returned to Harvard in 1840 as Hancock Professor of Hebrew and Dexter Professor of Sacred Literature, positions he occupied until his death in 1868.[9]

Prior to his Harvard appointment Noyes' public reputation rested on his translation of the Hebrew Scriptures.[10] His translation of Job, published in 1827, became the first in a series that eventually embraced all the Hebrew poetical books. Before coming to Harvard he had published new translations of the Psalms and Prophets, and in

[8] *Proverbs, Ecclesiastes, Canticles*, pp. 138–40.
[9] For biographical information on Noyes, see John C. Kimball, "George Rapall Noyes" in *Heralds of a Liberal Faith: The Preachers*, Samuel A. Eliot, ed. (3 vols.; Boston: American Unitarian Association, 1910), III, 269–74; and Joseph H. Allen, "George Rapall Noyes," *The Christian Examiner*, LXXXV (1868), 76–81.
[10] In addition to his *Proverbs, Ecclesiastes, and Canticles*, see his *An Amended Version of the Book of Job* (Cambridge: Hilliard and Brown, 1827); *A New Translation of the Hebrew Prophets* (3 vols.; Boston: James Munroe, 1837); *A New Translation of the Book of Psalms* (Boston: James Munroe, 1846).

1846 he completed his translations of Proverbs, Ecclesiastes, and Canticles. By means of these translations, augmented with introductions and notes, Noyes hoped to reach the general Christian community by affording laymen an opportunity to survey the results of biblical studies previously confined to the scholar's world and at the same time providing a readable version of the Old Testament. Furthermore, Noyes hoped he might prepare the way for the production of much needed critical commentaries on the Old Testament.[11]

Noyes persisted in his efforts to publish new translations of the Old Testament, even though the project became a financial burden to him. He explained to Andrews Norton that two years after the publication of his translation of the Prophets he was "$125 *out of pocket,* as they say." [12] He gave the translation of Job to the publisher in exchange for fifty copies of the book.[13] And on another occasion Norton provided funds to clear Noyes' account with his publisher. Noyes regarded the lack of interest in his translations as an omen of the times, and gloomily reported to Norton the observation of his bookseller that "15 or so years ago he sold 20 learned theological books where he sells one now." [14]

Noyes first ventured into theological polemics in a critical review of Hengstenberg's *Christology of the Old Testament,* published in the *Christian Examiner* of 1834.[15] Undoubtedly he was responding to Edward Robinson's sympathetic introduction of Hengstenberg in *The Biblical Repository.* Noyes' critique of the conservative German theologian included an explicit denial that Jesus had fulfilled any specific Old Testament prophecy. Because the argument of fulfilled prophecy had been a traditional proof for the truth of Christianity, the review caused a furor in the orthodox camp as well as in conservative Unitarian circles. The Attorney General of Massachusetts threatened to prosecute Noyes on a charge of blasphemy, a threat

[11] *Prophets,* I, vi, vii.
[12] Noyes to Norton, 4 June 1835.
[13] Noyes to Norton, 20 March 1837.
[14] Noyes to Norton, 21 February 1840.
[15] George R. Noyes, "Review of *Christology of the Old Testament* by E. W. Hengstenberg," *The Christian Examiner,* XVI (1834), 321–64. Hengstenberg was the leading biblical scholar of German orthodoxy and a professor at the University of Berlin.

which, although it never materialized, gave Noyes some notoriety as a liberal biblical scholar. Noyes feared that he might lose his parish, and communicated his fears to Norton.

> I had flattered myself that I had done a service to the cause of religion by an attempt to reconcile certain *facts* in regard to the prophecies of the [Old Testament] and the use made by them by writers in the New with the divine authority of Christ. But if such men as the Attorney General class such pieces as mine with the productions of [Abner] Kneeland & Fanny Wright, what is the encouragement for labouring to place Christianity on its true bases? My name has not yet been alluded to in connexion with the article, and I hope it will not be. The subject cannot be understood by common readers, and I am afraid my usefulness here in the country might be seriously affected, were it known that I had been denounced in such a style by one so high in authority as the Attorney General, a member of a Unitarian church. If the Editors of the Examiner choose to say anything on the subject I hope I shall be kept out of sight; for possibly such a use might be made of the article as to deprive me of employment and my family of bread.[16]

Noyes did not feel that the proofs from prophecy were needed to substantiate the Christian faith. Indeed, such proofs had been an embarrassment in the past, for sceptics had demonstrated the inadequacy of the argument and turned it against the Christian faith. Modifying the traditional Lockean position of New England liberals, he maintained that Jesus, an inspired prophet from God, had taught the supernatural truths essential to Christianity and had authenticated his teaching by miracles. The teaching of Jesus and the report of the substantiating miracles had been communicated to succeeding generations by "contemporaneous history"; arguments about fulfilled prophecy should be renounced.[17]

Noyes did not deny that Jesus was the Messiah. Rather, he asserted that Jesus had truly defined the meaning of the title by "accomplish[ing] purposes of God, and . . . [by] introduc[ing] a dispensation, for which the whole Jewish economy had been a prepa-

[16] Noyes to Norton, 11 July 1831.
[17] "Hengstenberg," p. 324.

ration . . . ." [18] The fact was that the Old Testament messianic expectation had been extremely vague and erroneously conceived. Old Testament prophets had anticipated a Messiah-king who would establish God's rule over all the earth by making all nations subservient to Israel.[19] Their predictions could not be reconciled with the actual history of Jesus.

Hengstenberg had supposed that prophetic language conveyed a double sense: the lower level of meaning, represented by the literal significance of prophetic writings; the higher, and true, level of meaning, represented by the way in which the prophecy had been fulfilled. Hence, Hengstenberg conceived that God had inspired Old Testament prophets to utter truths, truths of which they were totally unaware and the meaning of which remained covert until they were fulfilled in Jesus Christ.[20]

Noyes did not attempt to conceal his contempt for Hengstenberg's pretentious scholarship. "He possesses but a feeble capacity of reasoning concerning the meaning of words, or the relations of things." [21] His fame, Noyes thought, stemmed from his zealous effort to "resuscitate the dry bones of Lutheran orthodoxy," but the extravagant theories he imposed upon Scripture were as ridiculous and dangerous as those of any sceptical rationalist. His arguments were so much "learned dust" raised to obscure critical problems.[22]

The Old Testament writings, argued Noyes, could have only one meaning, the meaning intended by the writer. Responsible exegesis of the Old Testament Prophets and Psalms, based on the principles employed in recovering the meaning of other ancient writings, amply demonstrated that Jewish writers before the time of Jesus conceived of the Messiah in terms of a conquering king. Their prophecies could not have applied to Jesus, who established a spiritual kingdom on the basis of his religious teaching.

Noyes admitted that New Testament writers appealed to fulfilled

[18] "Hengstenberg," p. 327.

[19] "Hengstenberg," p. 333.

[20] Even Moses Stuart found this idea untenable. See his "On the Alleged Obscurity of Prophecy," *American Biblical Repository,* II (1832), 217–45.

[21] "Hengstenberg," p. 321.

[22] "Hengstenberg," p. 320.

Old Testament prophecy as a means of confirming the truth of Christianity. But in so doing they distorted the true meaning of the Old Testament. Apostles and Evangelists did not employ proper methods of exegesis; therefore their arguments must be rejected.

In his scathing review of Hengstenberg Noyes was moved by two concerns. First, he desired to base his defense of Christianity on unassailable propositions.

> It appears to us that Christianity has suffered much from the connection with its defence, of propositions, which are untenable. The commonly received doctrine of the inspiration of all the writings included in the Bible, is a millstone hung round its neck, sufficient to sink it. That Christianity has been able to sustain, not only itself, but the mighty mass of errors, which have been connected with it, from the time of the Judaizing Christians to the present day, is a fact which speaks strongly of the strength of its evidence.[23]

The proposition that Jesus literally fulfilled the prophecies of the Old Testament impeded the progress of Christian truth. It must be excised.

Noyes' second concern was the defense of the authority of revelation.

> Human reason must necessarily be the interpreter of the Bible. If this reason, exercised in subjection to established laws of interpretation, bring us to conclusions different from those to which the Apostles arrived, we cannot give them up without undermining the authority of Revelation. For how do we know that we understand the meaning of any interpretation of a passage by the Apostles? How, but by the exercise of our reason?[24]

Any revelation that must be supported by alien and unreasonable theories, such as those presented by Hengstenberg, could be no revelation at all.

Noyes came to Harvard in 1840 upon the personal recommendation of Andrews Norton.[25] He succeeded John Gorham Palfrey, who

[23] "Hengstenberg," p. 357.

[24] "Hengstenberg," pp. 355–56.

[25] See Norton's undated letter to President Quincy in Letter Book B, pp. 188–92.

had taught the biblical courses since Norton's resignation in 1830. Palfrey had apparently been an adequate teacher and scholar, although in no way especially remarkable. His published lectures reveal a broad familiarity with current trends in biblical scholarship, but he himself tended to be more conservative than either Norton or Noyes, and the general tenor of his lectures was homiletic and apologetic rather than critical.[26]

Palfrey located the religious authority of the Old Testament in the Mosaic revelation of monotheism and moral law. It was verified, he thought, by miracles; indeed, he could conceive of no other way of verifying revelation. Consequently, he maintained, the Pentateuch possessed the same authority within the Old Testament as the Gospels within the New. Thus, Palfrey conceived that the Bible contained two supernatural revelations of God, and he spoke of two supernatural dispensations, one of Moses and the other of Jesus. The revelation of God through Jesus superseded the Mosaic revelation, which was less complete and was adapted to the immaturity of the human race.[27] Like Moses Stuart, Palfrey regarded most of the Pentateuch as a journal of Moses, although he readily admitted the presence of numerous glosses by later hands.[28] Moses had composed Genesis as an introduction to the Pentateuch to give the people who received the law and the land of Palestine their historical traditions in a convenient form. But in doing so he was acting as an "uninspired compiler" and had used at least two ancient sources.[29]

[26] On Palfrey, see Frank Otto Gatell, *John Gorham Palfrey and the New England Conscience* (Cambridge: Harvard University Press, 1963). Palfrey's lectures on the Old Testament were published as *Academical Lectures on the Jewish Scriptures and Antiquities* (4 vols.; Boston: James Munroe, 1838–1852).

[27] See *Academical Lectures,* I, pp. 1, 71; II, p. vi; and throughout Lectures 8 and 9.

[28] See particularly *Academical Lectures,* I, 194, for Palfrey's argument that the tradition of the pre-Mosaic sabbath was the result of a gloss.

[29] *Academical Lectures,* II, 2–31. Palfrey's position was identical to Jean Astruc's; although he was familiar with De Wette's late dating of Deuteronomy, he refused to accept that hypothesis or to recognize the continuation of sources throughout the Pentateuch.

Except for the Pentateuch, Palfrey felt free to be critical: he claimed that the later books were historically accurate and evaluated their religious significance by the degree to which they conformed to the Mosaic revelation. On the question of prophecy Palfrey followed Noyes, noting that Jesus himself had defined the nature of the messianic office and contending that the prophets in their speculation had generally misconceived the plans of God.[30]

Both Noyes and Norton were displeased with Palfrey's performance at the Divinity School. In a letter to Norton Noyes explained that, having known several recent graduates of the Divinity School, he was convinced that one reason for religious unrest among the young liberals was "the want of confidence in the exposition of the present professor [Palfrey] and the want of respect for him *as a teacher*."[31] Behind the scenes, Norton worked to replace Palfrey with Noyes. However, Palfrey himself was ready to launch his political career (he was elected to the Massachusetts legislature in 1842) and resigned in 1839, leaving the way clear for Noyes' appointment.

Noyes did not assume his new duties at the Divinity School without misgivings. He confided his anxieties to Andrews Norton in the summer of 1839.

I hardly know what is best for myself personally, or what are my wishes, in relation to the subject. Twelve years ago, I left Cambridge with great regret. I found great delight in studies connected with the Greek Tutorship, and in other studies, for which I found leisure. But in 12 years my feelings and habits have in some measure changed. I have become interested in the labors and duties of the Christian ministry; I have found happiness in endeavoring to discharge my duties to the people of a country parish, and even the hills and valleys, among which I have lived so long, have acquired such charms for me, that, if I ever part from them, I shall part from them with regret. On the other hand, I find more satisfaction in Biblical studies than in the composition of sermons or in pastoral duties; and should be glad of

[30] *Academical Lectures,* II, 358 ff.
[31] Noyes to Norton, 1 June 1839.

an opportunity of devoting more time to such studies, and of obtaining access to greater facilities for pursuing them. And this is nearly all that makes the Heb[rew] professorship desirable to me.[32]

Noyes' apprehensions were well founded. Until 1857 he shared the entire teaching responsibility with only one other professor, assuming the courses in Old and New Testament and half of the courses in theology and ecclesiastical history, as well as the duties of the College Preacher. It seemed to Noyes that the Divinity School would either limp along with two professors or be discontinued altogether. His dedication probably maintained the institution throughout this period of decline, which saw few students seeking admission, fewer pursuing ministerial careers after graduation, and the general decay of academic and spiritual morale.[33] His demanding responsibilities at Harvard actually arrested his development as a publishing biblical scholar, but the manuscripts of his lectures afford a means of assessing his position concerning biblical research.[34]

Noyes was a loyal pupil of Andrews Norton. His Christian faith was firmly grounded in the belief that Jesus Christ was a messenger sent from God, an inspired prophet who taught the authoritative principles of true religion. His office had been authenticated by miracles; the miracles and teaching had been reported accurately by the contemporary witnesses who had written the four Gospels. The Gospels were absolutely genuine and contained only the minor discrepancies, which demonstrated that they had been written by four independent authors. All four could be harmonized in such a way that the scholar could see a reliable sketch of the course of Christ's ministry.

He maintained, however, that the teaching of Christ carried divine authority only in the moral and religious realm. In a course on the Old Testament prophets Noyes told his students:

[32] Noyes to Norton, 13 June 1839.

[33] Noyes to Norton, 15 May 1840; see also, Sydney E. Ahlstrom, "The Middle Period (1840–80)," in *The Harvard Divinity School,* George Huntston Williams, ed. (Boston: Beacon, 1954), pp. 78–147.

[34] Noyes' lectures (MSS in the Harvard University Archives; microfilm copy in the Princeton University Library), will be referred to by title and number.

My own impression is, that if the Evangelists have reported correctly the language of Jesus, then he must have used typical or allegorical interpretation, and have supposed that passages in the O[ld] T[estament] had a real relation to himself. And if the report is correct, Jesus was in error.[35]

Never had a Unitarian biblical scholar argued more persistently for the proper role of reason in apprehending the revelation of God. Every man, through the faculty of his reason, received a direct revelation from God, by which he could understand the *"primary* truths of religion," and the *"elementary* principles of duty." [36] Reason was "the best gift of God to man"; Jesus could not limit the scope of its inquiry.[37]

The content of the revelation that God gave directly to every man through the faculties of his reason was an inadequate foundation for true religion. To that natural revelation must be added the content of a supernatural revelation, as found in the Bible.

The word of God is the truth which God communicated to mankind by his messengers, especially by Jesus Christ, or by the Holy Spirit to the individual soul. The Scriptures are the records of the word of God, and of many other things besides.[38]

The reasonable apprehension of truth common to every man had been heightened by the spirit of God in some men to such an extent that they had received a supernatural revelation, but such inspiration made neither the men nor their writings infallible.[39]

Noyes rejected any notion of a progressive revelation in the Old Testament. God's revelation of truth had remained constant throughout human history. Men had continually mingled God's revealed truth with myths and legends, with fallible predictions and erroneous opinions. The problem for the nineteenth-century Christian was to separate the unchangeable truths of revelation from the human accretions in which they were embodied.[38]

---

[35] "Prophets," Lecture XIII.
[36] "Prophets," Lecture XV.
[37] "Prophets," Lecture I.
[38] "Pentateuch," Lecture I.
[39] "Prophets," Lecture XIV.

Like his mentor, Andrews Norton, Noyes found the primary locus of Christian truth in the Gospels. But he maintained that the rational Christian must also study the Old Testament, because Christianity was founded on the "essential principles" of Judaism.[40] Jesus had come to perfect, not destroy, the Law and the Prophets.

The primary task of the biblical critic was to recover the meaning of the scriptural writings. In this task he must employ all the scientific tools of historical and literary criticism. He must always keep in mind the fact that a writing could have only one meaning, the meaning assigned by the author. Once the original meaning had been recovered one might decide whether it represented an eternal truth revealed by God or merely a human opinion.

Noyes was truly concerned to preserve the "otherness" of the Bible. In his lectures on Genesis he severely condemned pious scientists who attempted to reconcile the biblical account of creation with modern discovery. The Bible must be allowed to mean what it actually says about creation, namely, that the world was created in six ordinary days and that the firmament was a solid substance that could retain heavenly waters. Scientists might demonstrate that these biblical conceptions were naive and mistaken, but the writing must be given the clear meaning of its author.

> If we undertake to interpret the Scriptures in any other mode, or by any other principles, than those by which other writings are interpreted, we give up the Scriptures to the fancy or fanaticism of the reader. We thus take away all authority from any part of it. And allegory in this respect stands on precisely the same footing as rationalism.[41]

Noyes could not conceive of himself as a rationalist, for in his view the rationalists were those who rejected all possibility of divine intervention, all possibility of supernaturalism. But, although he was a supernaturalist, he was also a rationalist. The core of his Christian faith lay in the truths that Jesus taught. When Jesus taught something unreasonable, however, such as the existence of demons or fulfillment of Old Testament prophecies, he either erred or adapted

40 "Pentateuch," Lecture I.
41 "Pentateuch," Lecture IV.

himself to the prejudices of his audience. Noyes accepted the Bible
as authoritative divine revelation. But when the Bible disagreed with
his rational comprehension of eternal truth, it was presenting human
opinion rather than eternal verities. In short, although Noyes preserved the "otherness" of the Bible, he could not preserve the "otherness" of revelation. He had accepted the great truths as a pious, but
liberal, nineteenth-century rationalist.

Noyes was precluded from becoming a significant force in the
spread of critical studies in America. The teaching demands of his
position prohibited extensive publication, and the number of his students was too small to transmit his influence to the liberal community. He was remarkably conversant with the progress of German
biblical studies and in his Old Testament lectures consistently
adopted the progressive views of pioneering scholars such as De
Wette and Kuenen. Critical studies, however, could not shake his
adherence to the conservative position of Andrews Norton on the
New Testament.[42]

Noyes recognized the waning interest in biblical studies among
New England liberals. In an address delivered to the Divinity School
alumni in 1847, he discussed this decline and suggested some reasons
for it.[43] Noyes identified the apparent success of the movement in
biblical studies as a prominent cause of its decline. American church-
men, with some justifiable pride, could point to the accomplishments
of their scholars. Within his lifetime Noyes had observed the renewed interest in the biblical languages, demonstrated by the appearance of several grammars and lexicons, which had been successfully
sold and reprinted. Translations of important German works and
American commentaries, "which, though not of first-rate excellence
and likely to stand the test of time, are certainly in advance of the
popular English commentaries," testified to the recognized importance of biblical studies in this country.[44] But the seminaries, which
had fostered the growth of biblical studies, lacked the means to con-

[42] See his lectures on the Gospel of John.
[43] The address, "Causes of the Decline of Interest in Critical Theology,"
was published in the *Christian Examiner,* XLIII (1847), 325-44.
[44] "Decline," pp. 325-26.

tinue and were failing for lack of public support.[45] Although many of the ominous-looking problems of early days had been successfully solved, Noyes enumerated five problems that needed immediate attention: 1) the authority and meaning of both the Old and New Testaments; 2) the connection between the Old and the New Testament; 3) the nature of prophecy; 4) the Christology of the Old Testament; and 5) the eschatology of Jesus and the Apostles. Noyes thought the need for research obvious.

> Of this every one must be convinced who reflects that there exists not a respectable commentary on the Old Testament in the English language . . . and none on the New Testament at all corresponding to the wants of the times. . . .[46]

Noyes astutely noted the quickened interest in problems of social reform among the clergy. Though he praised this social concern, he felt that too much activism might lead to the erosion of the intellectual traditions of Christianity.[47]

Because the Bible was no longer universally recognized as the infallibly inspired word of God, many thought that its study was of little importance. This was particularly evident among those "who deny any peculiar authority even to the declarations of Jesus Christ. . . ."[47] Noyes countered by pointing to the high esteem in which Christians regarded the Bible, to its pervasive influence, and to its intrinsic value.

With obvious reference to the Transcendentalists, Noyes attributed the decline of bliblical studies in part to "a prevalent notion of universal inspiration, or intuitive perception, extending not merely to the first principles of faith, but to nearly all truth on all subjects" [48] Noyes felt that those who thought they could immediately apprehend all truth were not likely to labor with interpretative principles and ancient texts.

But the greatest cause of waning interest Noyes attributed to disillusionment. The liberals had begun their biblical studies hoping to find a critical tool that would force the reform of New England the-

---

[45] "Decline," p. 327.
[46] "Decline," p. 335.
[47] "Decline," p. 331.
[48] "Decline," p. 339.

ology and restore the pure Christianity of the New Testament. The anticipated goal had not been realized. Nor had the pursuit of biblical studies been effective in winning sceptics to Christianity. Indeed, many thought biblical studies *responsible* for the growth of a new scepticism. Noyes admitted that the faith of many Christians had been disturbed when they realized that the Bible was not the infallible revelation of God. However, such a disturbance should not be attributed to biblical studies, but rather to the absurdity of the doctrine of scriptural infallibility. Christianity must be able to "progress in the truth," though it disturb the faith of many.[49]

Noyes remained firmly convinced of the great importance of critical biblical studies. He had begun his career during the more promising days of the American movement and sadly observed the declining interest in the subject. As a final monument to his conviction the American Unitarian Association published his translation of the New Testament from Tischendorf's Greek text in 1869. Noyes completed this last effort of biblical translation in 1868, only a few days prior to his death.

[49] "Decline," pp. 333-35.

CHAPTER IX

THE FOREIGN INVASION

D. F. *Strauss's* Life of Jesus *in America*

WHEN George R. Noyes addressed the alumni of the Harvard Divinity School in 1847 in an appeal for renewed interest in biblical studies among the liberals, he made extensive reference to one particular work of German scholarship, D. F. Strauss's *Life of Jesus*. Like later historians, Noyes seemed to realize that Strauss's book was one of the most important works of biblical criticism of the first half of the nineteenth century. It was a study that no biblical scholar could ignore.

By 1847 the *Life of Jesus* was already a well-known work in America.[1] It had been noticed in American periodicals as early as 1839, two years following its German publication, and, by the time Noyes' speech appeared in the *Christian Examiner* in 1847, reviews of Strauss's book by Theodore Parker, Stephen G. Bulfinch, and George E. Ellis had also appeared there. Strauss's work was so widely recognized in America as early as 1846 that Ellis felt it necessary to explain to his readers that it had originated in Germany and *not* in America.[2] Noyes felt, however, that the American response to Strauss was both deficient and uncritical; he had good reason.

Theodore Parker, who first reviewed the work for the *Christian Examiner*,[3] had been mainly concerned to give an exposition of *Das*

---

[1] See Henry A. Pochman, *German Culture in America* (Madison: University of Wisconsin Press, 1961), pp. 111–12.

[2] On the other hand, Strauss was little reviewed in England. Only one article on him appeared during the decade of the forties, and that was a comparison of Strauss and Theodore Parker. See J. Estlin Carpenter, *The Bible in the Nineteenth Century* (London: Longmans, Green, and Co., 1903), pp. 242, 283.

[3] "D. F. Strauss's *Das Leben Jesu*," XXVIII (1840), 273–316.

Leben Jesu. Stephen G. Bulfinch, whose review appeared in 1845,[4] attempted to be more critical, but could not escape his pious religious feelings. Bulfinch praised Strauss's courage and candor, and his thorough annihilation of the naturalistic explanation of Gospel miracles. But, agreeing with many contemporary German critics, he felt that Strauss's book only demonstrated how ridiculous biblical criticism could become when carried to extremes. Nothing Strauss had said shook Bulfinch's faith in the authenticity of the Gospels, and although he admitted that they contained many discrepancies, he felt they only substantiated the independent character of the four authors, who had been either direct witnesses of Christ or the intimate followers of the Apostles. He completely rejected on the grounds of his own rational experience Strauss's rigorous application of myth to the Gospel narratives: men of his own day could not conceivably think of the War of 1812, an event that had taken place thirty years ago, in mythological terms; therefore it was unreasonable to contend that the authors of the New Testament could have applied myth to the history of Jesus after a similar period of time.

Bulfinch, like most American Christians, would not subject the Bible to scholarly criticism if it threatened his faith. He wrote:

> Truly, if the *caput mortuum* of Christianity which mythicism leaves us, be all that is true of our religion, our feelings would tempt us to forgive the Evangelists who have so beautifully deceived rather than the critics who so coldly disenchant us.[5]

The beauty of a religious faith founded on the authenticity of the Gospels and on the divine mission of Jesus authenticated by miracles could not be threatened by the meticulous researches of a biblical critic.

George E. Ellis assumed a similar position in his review of Strauss, published in 1846.[6] Convinced that excessive effort had been invested

[4] "Strauss's Life of Jesus:—The Mythic Theory," XXXIX (1845), 145–69. For a biographical sketch of Bulfinch, see *Lamb's Biographical Dictionary of the United States,* John Howard Brown, ed. (Boston: Lamb, 1900), I, 485.
[5] "The Mythic Theory," p. 160.
[6] "The Mythical Theory Applied to the Life of Jesus," *Christian Examiner,* XLI (1846), 313. For a biographical sketch of Ellis, see James Truslow Adams, *Dictionary of American Biography* (New York: Scribner's, 1931), VI, 103–04.

in biblical criticism, Ellis observed that too many biblical critics were motivated by a destructive spirit. He extolled the Christian preachers, who in contrast spent as much time in the study of the Gospels as any biblical critic, but produced "practical applications of spiritual lessons" rather than sceptical treatises.[7]

Like Bulfinch, Ellis could not conceive that myth could have been applied to the history of Jesus in so short a period of time or that the discrepancies among the Gospels could indicate anything more than the independence of four honest testimonies. Ellis could not account for all the errors of the Gospels, but he could point to the learned study of Andrews Norton, who had rationally upheld the genuineness of the Gospels and had dealt adequately with all the discrepancies which he could discover. One could not reconstruct a chronological history of the ministry of Jesus, for the Gospels represented a "transfer to parchment of the preaching of the Apostles"; but there was no need to doubt the truth of apostolic preaching or the historicity of Jesus.

Ellis thought Strauss's book should be ignored because it was the natural result of the reckless and sceptical philosophy of Germany. "He has . . . given us the summing up of a whole mass of mutually conflicting and almost equally worthless speculations."[8] American Unitarians who followed the line laid down by Andrews Norton would accept no biblical critcism that strayed from the philosophical presuppositions of John Locke.

Noyes was satisfied neither with brief American critiques of Strauss nor with the more extensive refutations produced in Germany. He found Strauss's Hegelianism no more palatable than did other Americans, but he recognized that Strauss's work should be judged as the labor of a competent biblical scholar. Strauss's scepticism was the natural product of a philosophy that excluded all possibility of miracle. The scepticism could be refuted by good common sense, but the scholarly criticism Strauss had applied to the Gospels could only be refuted by an equally competent scholarship.[9]

[7] "The Mythical Theory Applied," pp. 347–48.

[8] "The Mythical Theory Applied," p. 368.

[9] George R. Noyes, "Causes of the Decline of Interest in Critical Theology," *Christian Examiner*, XLIII (1847), 338.

Noyes lamented that Americans were prejudiced against critical studies and that they would not support a scholarly community capable of meeting Strauss on his own ground. "We do need an answer to a work so learned and plausible as Strauss's Life of Jesus," he argued.

> Let those . . . who condemn critical studies . . . tell us how long it is desirable that the most elaborate exposition of the life of the Founder of Christianity should be the production of one who denies the divinity of his mission.[10]

Specifically, Noyes called for an American work of scholarship and learning, a critical life of Jesus or a commentary on the Gospels that could be recognized by the entire scholarly world.

Perhaps Andrews Norton heard Noyes' address and felt the challenge of Noyes' remarks. Norton could not take Strauss seriously because Strauss was obviously unacquainted with the three volumes on *The Genuineness of the Gospels*. Norton felt he had proved that the Gospels were written by the authors whose names they bore, two of whom were eyewitnesses to the ministry of Jesus and the other two companions of Apostles. Strauss's assumption that the Gospels were written not by the apostolic community, but by naïve disciples dominated by a mythological outlook, simply could not be reconicled with the facts and arguments Norton had demonstrated in his own major work; he thought he had left Strauss no ground to stand upon. However, in 1847 and 1848, after the English translation of Strauss's work had appeared, he wrote an elaborate refutation, and in 1855 it was published posthumously as part of *Internal Evidences of the Genuineness of the Gospels*.[11]

The real disparity between Strauss and Norton lay in their views of history. From his Hegelian philosophy Strauss derived an important critical principle of historical research: forms and modes of thought differ from age to age. Before the critical historian could attempt to reconstruct the past, he must understand the presuppositions and conceptual modes of the era he wished to interpret. The scholar

[10] "Decline," p. 343.
[11] Boston: Little, Brown, 1855, p. 18.

of the nineteenth century did not share common conceptual modes with the authors of the Gospels. For the writer of the first century myths and legends were common modes of expression, and in using myth they were neither fabricating falsehood nor describing events in a scientific manner. The problem for the New Testament scholar was to translate the substance of myth and legend into discursive scientific history.[12]

Strauss was certain that scientific history was history written within the guidelines of Hegel's philosophy. Consequently, the central truth behind all the myths of the Gospels was the idea of the incarnation of God in man, a manifestation of the eternal spirit's motion in terms of thesis, antithesis, and synthesis. The major strength of Strauss's *Life of Jesus* was his understanding of the historiographical problem involved in reconstructing first-century Christianity. The major weakness, for all but Hegelians, was the interpretation of the past in the categories of a philosophical system.

Norton assumed that the presuppositions and conceptual modes of the first century were essentially similar to those of the nineteenth. Therefore he felt he could rely upon his sources to have performed the critical function of historical analysis. That is to say, Norton imagined that the authors of the Gospels and the community that accepted them acted as he would have done had he actually been present. To be sure, he recognized that although he was better educated than the founders of Christianity and was not a part of their Jewish world, they were no less reasonable than he. Had they been unethical men, the authors of the New Testament might have purposely perpetrated false fables, but they would scarcely have been able to found a great religion on the basis of falsehood. As rational and ethical men, therefore, they had exercised their critical powers and had accurately reported the teaching of Jesus and the miracles that proved Jesus spoke with the authority of one sent from God. If some early Christians had embellished the story of Jesus with myth and legend,

[12] The dependence of Strauss on Hegel and Strauss's use of myth are complex problems. For a recent discussion of these issues, see Van A. Harvey, "D. F. Strauss' *Life of Jesus* Revisited," *Church History*, XXX (1961), 191–211; see also, Albert Schweitzer, *The Quest of the Historical Jesus* (New York: Macmillan Paperbacks, 1961), pp. 68–121.

the Apostles would necessarily have corrected their errors. That the Gentiles, who had little respect for the Jews, could have accepted Christianity proved to Norton that the Gospels were historically reliable, for he assumed that the Gentiles used their rational critical powers to determine the validity of the Christian religion and of the Gospels that testified of Christ.

Norton had a further quarrel with the critical assumptions he attributed to Strauss. In the first place, he thought Strauss supposed he was dealing only with a problem in human history. In the second place, he thought that Strauss assumed *a priori* that miracle was impossible. Norton thought that before this second assumption could be maintained it must be established either that no power existed capable of performing miracles or that, if such a power did exist, it would never exercise itself.[13] And, if the first assumption were attacked, it would not be possible to maintain the second by appealing only to human history. Norton, then, wished to shift the ground of discussion from human history to theology: he did not wish to discuss events in human history but rather the being and nature of God. Actually, Norton was wrong about the second assumption he attributed to Strauss, for Strauss held, on *a posteriori* grounds, that miracle was impossible: he excluded miracle because he knew of no rational and critical man who claimed to have witnessed such an event. His *Life of Jesus* was therefore scientific enough. But Norton's theological approach to history offered him the ground for attacking and rejecting Strauss.

Equally incomprehensible to Norton was Strauss's effort to restore dogmatically to Christian theology what had been destroyed critically. Norton, whose philosophic heroes were Locke, Berkeley, and Butler, could not imagine a viable philosophy not grounded in empirical fact. Norton considered Hegel an atheist. Both Hegel and Strauss belonged to an ancient debased tradition that Norton called "the School of the Mystics," or the "School of the Incomprehensible." All Germany had become infected with obscurantist philosophy, which no man of good common sense could accept.[14]

13 *Internal Evidences,* p. 66.
14 *Internal Evidences,* pp. 147–68.

Norton's basic reaction to Strauss took three forms: a return to the incontrovertible evidence he had produced in *The Genuineness of the Gospels,* an attempt to refute Strauss's critical methods, and a contemptuous exposition of German philosophy in general and Hegelianism in particular. With characteristic thoroughness Norton attempted to refute in detail many of the positions taken by Strauss in the *Life of Jesus.*

Strauss had made extensive use of an assumed body of messianic myths, which he conceived had been applied to Jesus in the period between his death and the destruction of Jerusalem. The popular myths and fables had been applied to Jesus, not by the Apostles but by naïve Jewish believers and had later become a part of the Gospel tradition. Strauss had certainly over-extended himself in this argument, and Norton quickly discovered its weakness. While Strauss's view of Jewish messianic expectation was too broad, Norton's was too narrow. Norton restricted the scope of Jewish messianic expectation to the Messiah-king. Since Jesus had not presented himself in this character, but had explicitly contradicted its main features, Norton thought he could not have been described in terms of Jewish messianism, mythical or not.

It seemed to Norton that Strauss meant to deny all historicity to the Gospels. It was easy to read him this way. As Schweitzer points out,

> The tendency of the work to purely critical analysis, the ostentatious avoidance of any positive expression of opinion, and not least, the manner of regarding the Synoptics as mere bundles of narratives and discourses, make it difficult—indeed, strictly speaking, impossible— to determine Strauss' own distinctive conception of the life of Jesus, to discover what he really thinks is moving behind the curtain of myth.[15]

Norton was prepared to admit discrepancies and contradictions within the Gospels, but he thought the "essential truth" of the narratives unimpaired by them. Like contemporary German critics, he attempted to demonstrate that Strauss's critical methods made the

---

[15] Schweitzer, *Quest,* p. 90.

writing of all history impossible. Turning to an event of secular history, the assassination of Caesar, Norton attempted a *reductio ad absurdum*.[16] But the attempt and the event were ill-chosen: the ancient testimony of Caesar's death only made more evident the fact that the historian *must* critically analyze his sources, rather than demonstrating that critical analysis made the writing of history impossible.

Andrews Norton, the guardian of Unitarian orthodoxy, assured his followers of the truth of his established position. His own position had remained unchanged in the face of Strauss's radical *Life of Jesus*. The principle of Unitarian theological authority was well established.

> The Gospels are the history of a miraculous communication from God to men. . . . [I]t relates to an event of inconceivable interest and importance. The Infinite Being has suspended the ordinary operations of his power to manifest himself more immediately to the dwellers on earth. The essential value of Christianity consists in its being such a revelation of Him. . . . If God has thus revealed his existence and his purposes towards us, the truths of religion rest on an immovable basis,—the witness of God himself.[17]

For Norton the battle had been fought and the victory won. He died in 1852, never doubting that he had guided the New England liberals toward the pure Christianity of the New Testament.[18]

Strauss's *Life of Jesus* generated very little interest among the con-

---

[16] *Internal Evidences,* pp. 70–82.

[17] *Internal Evidence,* pp. 126–27.

[18] A position very similar to Norton's was taken by one of his former students, W. H. Furness, a Philadelphia Unitarian minister. In the introduction to his *History of Jesus* (Boston: Crosby, Nichols, and Co., 1853) p. vi, he wrote: "Considering now how writers of great erudition and acuteness are maintaining that the accounts of Christ are mere collections of myths, it is interesting to find how even imperfect attempts as I have made to ascertain the truth of the Gospels from their internal character result in substantiating the main facts of these histories." Furness earlier had relinquished the traditional postion that the miracles verified the supernatural revelation of Jesus, although he still thought them credible. See Furness, *Remarks on the Four Gospels* (Philadelphia: Carey, Lea, and Blanchard, 1836.) Although he was frequently classified with the Transcendentalists, his appreciation of Strauss was not as warm as Parker's.

servative party of New England Congregationalism. Between 1839 and 1847 the *Christian Examiner* devoted 123 pages to commentary on Strauss and his work. In the corresponding conservative journals, the *American Biblical Repository* and *Bibliotheca Sacra,* scarcely any notice is taken of Strauss. The conservatives were willing to let the Unitarians refute the new German heresy. For years Moses Stuart had been predicting that radical German criticism would invade America, that irreligious Americans would welcome scholarly support for their scepticism, and that conservatives must prepare for the great conflict if they hoped to make America a religious nation. The invasion had come, but, contrary to Stuart's expectations, the most radical German critic made no American converts. Even the liberals would not accept him.

Ralph Waldo Emerson had succeeded in his Divinity School address of 1838 in forcing traditional Unitarians to face a division within their own camp. In that address Emerson criticized the cold, logical formalism of a system of belief based upon a revelation of divine truth through Jesus and authenticated by miracles. In its place he advocated a religion based upon the immediate reception of spiritual truth. Orthodox Unitarians, especially Andrews Norton, could not tolerate such criticism of their rational position. Consequently, the conservatives enjoyed a period of peace, while Emerson's followers —the Transcendentalists—and traditional Unitarians fought their own battles.[19]

It is doubtful whether Moses Stuart had read Strauss or even mastered the secondary literature about the controversy that Strauss generated.[20] Stuart felt no need to enter the battle, because he could point to Theodore Parker, the Transcendentalists' spokesman on biblical criticism, as the most sceptical critic in America. "Beyond Mr. Par-

[19] See William R. Hutchinson, *The Transcendentalist Ministers* (New Haven: Yale University Press, 1959).

[20] In a sweeping condemnation of radical German opinion, Stuart referred to Strauss's work on the Gospels as being founded on a theory of "moral romance." This would seem a peculiar choice of words for one who possessed much knowledge of the work. Probably Stuart was quoting some secondary source, and that not a very knowledgeable one. See his *Miscellanies* (Andover: Allen, Morrill, and Wardwell, 1846), p. 195.

ker's position, we in this country, as I am inclined to think, cannot well go," he wrote. "It needs a *German* mind and education to do this." [21] But he continued with this ominous word of warning:

> But when the mass of the Unitarian party shall be led to occupy his [Parker's] ground, (which can hardly fail to take place), we shall then know where we are; and if we must take the field of contest, we shall know at least what fashion of armour we are to cope with, who our opponents are, and what kind of defensive or assailing weapons may be expedient on our part.[21]

Unlike Noyes, Stuart could not understand that biblical criticism had ceased to appear as dangerous a weapon as it once had.

No one in New England knew more about Strauss and the issues *Das Leben Jesu* than Theodore Parker. Quite possibly, Parker had secured the first copy of Strauss's work brought to the United States in 1836 or 1837.[22] By 1838, Parker was talking to Channing about the advisability of preparing an English translation of the work.[23] Channing discouraged the project, and Parker gave it up but continued to study and reflect upon the work of the German critic. A journal entry reflects some of Parker's difficulty with Strauss. Myths were the product of an age in which people did not think historically. Was the age of primitive Christianity unhistorical? This seemed to be an unresolved question in Parker's mind. But, he reflected, "no man can justly believe in myths in the New Testament who does not deny the fact that it was written by contemporaries or eyewitnesses." Strauss did deny that fact, and Parker seemed unwilling to agree.[24]

One cannot be certain that Parker's lengthy review of *Das Leben Jesu* for the *Christian Examiner* accurately represents his opinion

[21] *Miscellanies,* p. 196.

[22] See John White Chadwick, *Theodore Parker* (Boston: Houghton Mifflin, 1901), p. 88.

[23] Parker wrote in his journal, 19 April 1838: "Went to see Dr. Channing. Spoke about Strauss. He observed very archly he should not be *very* sorry if some of Kneeland's [famous Boston sceptic] followers would do it into English. He would not advise me to do it." John Weiss, *Life and Correspondence of Theodore Parker* (2 vols.; New York: Appleton, 1864), I, 109.

[24] Octavius Brooks Frothingham, *Theodore Parker* (Boston: Osgood, 1874), pp. 92–93.

about the work. On April first, 1839, he wrote in his journal: "I could not say all I would say from the standpoint of 'The Examiner'—for this is not allowable,—but the most the readers of that paper will bear." [25] Perhaps Parker's first review had been rejected by the *Examiner,* and the extant review represents one modified to suit the *Examiner*'s readers.

The main body of Parker's review consisted of a chapter by chapter exposition of *Das Leben Jesu.* In the final ten pages he pointed out the "false principles, extreme conclusions, and extravagances" in Strauss's book. Specifically, Parker enumerated four basic weaknesses of Strauss's study.

Strauss had claimed that he pursued his study without presuppositions. Parker thought this both impossible and undesirable. It was clear that Strauss presupposed the impossibility of miracle. Furthermore, he has assumed that "the Idea precedes the man who is supposed to realize that idea; that many men, having a certain doctrine, gradually and in a natural manner, refer this doctrine to some historical person. . . ." [26] Finally, and Parker stressed this point, Strauss denied the possibility of any incarnation of God, "not even of what, in a human manner, we call his Love, or Holiness." [26]

The author of *Das Leben Jesu* had too easily concluded that the Gospels were not genuine, ignoring the mass of external evidence to the contrary.[27] Parker was pleased that in the third edition of the work Strauss had evidenced some misgivings about the spuriousness of John.[28]

Strauss had not, Parker objected, written in a proper religious spirit. Other German critics were as "bold, unsparing, and remorseless" as he, but always left the impression of their piety. To Parker the Bible was a religious document, and as such its study demanded a religious spirit.

Finally, Parker criticized Strauss for making too extensive a use

[25] Frothingham, *Parker,* p. 121.
[26] "Strauss Review," p. 307.
[27] "Strauss Review," p. 308.
[28] "Strauss Review," pp. 281–82.

of the category of myth. "He has looked so long at mythical stories, that . . . he can see nothing but myths wherever he turns his eye." Parker contended that "the New Testament always rests on historical ground, though it is not common historical ground, nor is it so rigidly historical that no legendary or mythical elements have entered it." [29] In short, Parker was ready to agree with Strauss that the presuppositions of an earlier age differed from those of the nineteenth century; the history of New Testament times could not be approached as though it were history of the recent past. But the conceptual modes of the New Testament period were not altogether mythological. The critic must separate history from myth and legend. Parker thought that if Strauss had understood that myth embodied historical fact and not merely an Idea, he would have completed his task more profitably.[29]

For all his criticism of Strauss's work, Parker admired the German scholar. He had no doubt that he was a true Christian, and thought he was more Christian in his scepticism than Hengstenberg in his orthodoxy.[29] In a paragraph of conditional praise, which must have shocked the more conservative Unitarians, Parker wrote:

> Before mankind could pass over the great chasm between the frozen realm of stiff supernaturalism, and lifeless rationalism, on the one side, and the fair domain of *free religious thought,* where the only *essential* creed is the Christian motto, "Be perfect, as your Father in Heaven is perfect," and the only *essential* form of Religion is Love to your neighbor as to yourself, and to God with the whole heart, mind, and soul, on the other,—some one must plunge in, devoting himself unconsciously, or even against his will, for the welfare of the race. This hard lot Strauss has chosen for himself, and done what many we fear wished, but none dared to do. His book, therefore, must needs be negative, destructive, and unsatisfactory. It pleases no one. It is colder than ice. It is the most melancholy book we ever read. All nature was dark to us as we closed and finished it.[30]

Parker praised Strauss for his destruction of the barriers to the life

[29] "Strauss Review," p. 309.
[30] "Strauss Review," p. 314.

of "free religious thought"; he condemned him for failing to infuse his study with the feeling and piety of true religion. Parker was ready to launch an attack on moribund systems of theology, whether Calvinist or Unitarian, using the tool of biblical criticism. The constructive task could be performed without the aid of the Bible.

CHAPTER X

THE ENEMY WITHIN

Theodore Parker as a Biblical Critic

THE review of Strauss's *Das Leben Jesu* represented Theodore Parker's first scholarly contribution to a major religious journal. The
erudition manifest in the review surprised none of his friends, for
Parker's thirst for knowledge had become almost legendary. Born
in 1810 into the large and frugal family of a New England farmer,
he won his education by his own hard efforts. In 1831 he completed
the work for the Harvard degree, but because he had been unable to
pay tuition fees and had not been in residence at the university but
at his Lexington home during the course of his studies, the degree
was withheld. For three years he supported himself by teaching, until, in 1834, he had saved enough to enter the Harvard Divinity
School.

Parker was so diligent in his pursuit of his studies that his classmates, while admiring his prodigious efforts, thought he was des-
tined to become a scholarly bookworm.[1] In one two-month period,
he read sixty-five books in five different languages and made copious
notes and summaries of them in his journal.[2]

The principal object of Parker's reading was the study of the Bible.
Even before entering the Divinity School he borrowed a number of
books from the library of Convers Francis and began "the great
study, the criticism of the New Testament."[3] The college library

---

[1] Octavius Brooks Frothingham, *Theodore Parker* (Boston: Osgood, 1874),
pp. 44–45.
[2] Frothingham, *Parker,* pp. 46–47.
[3] John Weiss, *Life and Correspondence of Theodore Parker* (2 vols.; New
York: Appleton, 1864), I, 64.

proved a great resource that Parker could not resist. He read widely in the Rabbinnic literature, the church fathers, and the modern German critics, seeking to understand the history of biblical interpretation.[4] He studied the Bible in its original languages and early versions and became so proficient in Hebrew that he taught the subject to Harvard undergraduates.[5]

As a student, Parker's opinions about the Bible adhered very closely to those of his professor, John Gorham Palfrey. While in the Divinity School he had concluded that the component books of the Bible were heterogenous, of dubious or anonymous authorship, and filled with many different doctrines. The Old Testament and the New even dealt with opposite kinds of religion. Furthermore, the books had been collected without reasonable or scientific method, so that the canon was an indiscriminate collection of books.[6] Miracles reported in the Bible presented special problems: Parker rejected those that seemed impossible, ridiculous, or wicked, but "still arbitrarily admitted others." [7] He specifically rejected the miracle of the virgin birth of Christ.[7] Parker surrendered any belief in the plenary, infallible, or verbal inspiration of the Scripture; and he even doubted that one could speak of the Scriptures as divinely inspired at all, since he "could not put [his] finger on any great moral or religious truth taught by revelation in the New Testament, which had not previously been set forth by men for whom no miraculous help was ever claimed." [8]

Parker found an extra outlet for his biblical studies in serving as an editor of *The Scriptural Interpreter*. The publication had been founded in 1831 by Ezra Stiles Gannett, Channing's assistant at the Federal Street Church, to promote family religious education in New England. Parker, with his classmates George E. Ellis and William Silsbee, assumed the responsibility for editing the magazine in 1835 while Gannett was in Europe. The three young editors attempted to

---

[4] Parker, *Theodore Parker's Experience as a Minister* (Boston: Leighton, 1860), p. 38.

[5] Frothingham, *Parker*, p. 47

[6] *Experience*, p. 39.

[7] *Experience*, p. 36.

[8] *Experience*, p. 37.

use the *Interpreter* as an organ to spread their new knowledge of the Bible throughout New England. Parker ambitiously translated Astruc's "Conjectures upon the Original Memoirs Which Moses Made Use of to Compose the Book of Genesis," [9] and the *Interpreter* frequently contained translations of an equally ambitious character from the writings of Eichhorn, Herder, Paulus, and other German critics.

The young scholars seemed to recognize that they had over-estimated the intellectual capacities of their readers. In the last number of the *Interpreter,* the editors explained:

> We have found our greatest difficulty to consist in deciding how far we might properly oppose popular opinions. Engaged as we have ourselves been, in the critical study of the scriptures, by the best helps which modern advancement has supplied, we have found many of our own early preconceived opinions to be untenable. We have seen good reasons for questioning even some of the most common grounds of reverence and faith supposed to be demanded by the scriptures. Rightfully, as we think, supposing that the respect which is founded upon blind error is superstition, we did not hesitate to withdraw our own when we found it had been unworthily bestowed. But how far were we to treat others as we treated ourselves? Here was the question which ofttimes perplexed us. . . . Much strong meat we had ourselves digested under the manly guidance of our loved and respected teachers, but we knew that there were babes who could bear nothing stronger than milk.[10]

Parker's views of the Bible expressed in the *Interpreter* were much more moderate than they were later to become. He defended the Mosaic authorship of the Pentateuch and told his readers that *"no man in the time of Moses could have devised such a code without miraculous aid."* [11] In spite of his personal doubts of the doctrine of biblical inspiration, he defended the doctrine in the *Interpreter* on the grounds of the great moral values to be found in Scripture. He regarded Paul as so inspired that he interpreted II Thessalonians 2:3 ("that day will not come, unless the rebellion comes first, and the

---

[9] *The Scriptural Interpreter,* VI (1836), 218–26; VII (1837), 23–37, 90–94.
[10] "Concluding Remarks," *The Scriptural Interpreter,* VII (1837), 285–88.
[11] "The Laws of Moses," *The Scriptural Interpreter,* VII (1837), 270.

man of lawlessness is revealed, the son of perdition") as a prediction of the papacy.[12] His first article for the *Interpreter* attempted to show that the Apostles had not predicted an imminent return of Jesus, since their whole authority would have been undermined had they been mistaken at this point.[13]

In the most daring article he wrote, "Translation and Exposition of Isaiah LII.13–LIII.12," Parker denied that Isaiah had predicted the ministry of Jesus, and asserted that the latter portion of the book was a pseudonymous writing.[14] That opinion was too radical for his audience. The following issue of the *Interpreter* contained a brief editorial note:

> The editors of the Interpreter received an anonymous letter a few weeks ago, complaining of the article upon Isaiah lii. and liii., and return their most hearty thanks for the kind caution, which the writer expressed with so Christian a spirit.[15]

Parker's views were slowly maturing. When Parker, Ellis, and Silsbee left the Divinity School in 1837, the *Interpreter* ceased publication. Parker's views of the Bible would thereafter be integrated with his pastoral ministry.

In 1837 Parker was settled as minister of the Unitarian congregation at West Roxbury. A letter written to Silsbee shortly after his ordination reveals Parker's search for an extra-biblical source and authority for his theology.

> To my mind . . . there is something strange and startling in the assertion, that man has been so constituted that he can, by the use of his faculties, on condition of obedience to their laws, achieve all the wonders of science and art, tell the dimensions of the planets and their whereabouts, and yet never be able by the use of his highest faculties— I mean the spontaneous religious sentiments—and by obedience to their laws, become able to learn religious truth, and to be certain it

[12] "Introduction to the Second Epistle to the Thessalonians," *The Scriptural Interpreter*, VI (1836), 65.
[13] "The Alleged Mistake of the Apostles," *The Scriptural Interpreter*, V (1835), 161–70.
[14] *The Scriptural Interpreter*, VI (1836), 174–90.
[15] *The Scriptural Interpreter*, VI (1836), 240.

was truth he learned and not error. Is it not most of all important for man to settle the questions of duty, to possess religious truth and religious life? Has God, so bountiful in bestowing other powers, given him none to discover those truths, the most important, the most necessary? . . . . Now, I believe God is the fountain of all Truth, which overflows from Him into all minds that lie low in his power, wishing to feed these minds of theirs in a wise passiveness; but how this influence comes, I do not know. I know nothing about the manner in which my soul is connected with God: I only know the fact. It is a matter of experience.[16]

As a parish minister Parker found his reverence for the Bible an embarrassment in his preaching. "I found this worship of the Bible . . . hindering me at each progressive step," he later recalled. His optimistic and progressive view of human nature was contradicted by both testaments. Biblical doctrines of hell, election, and damnation made it difficult to speak of God's universal love; the Bible made it appear that God "loved only a few, and them not overmuch." Parker wanted to encourage the free individuality of men's souls so that they might "all . . . be Christians as Jesus was a Christ," but instead the Bible enslaved men to absurd beliefs. Miracles violated the principles of natural law and made God seem capricious; furthermore, the Bible could even be cited in a way to make God the author of slavery.[17]

Parker's critical studies of the Bible could not but influence his preaching. From the beginning of his ministry he had discussed details of inconsistency in the Scripture and freely referred to some passages as flights of poetic fancy. He wrote two sermons which dealt at length with contradictions, inconsistencies, and historical error within the Bible, but hesitated over a year before delivering them. When he finally gave the sermons, he was relieved that the congregation gratefully received his attempt to "apply Common Sense to Religion and the Bible." [18]

[16] Parker to William Silsbee, 27 November 1838 in Weiss, *Parker,* I, 116–17.

[17] *Experience,* pp. 61–62.

[18] *Experience,* p. 61.

Parker's maturing views of the Bible, so cautiously disclosed to the small rural congregation at West Roxbury, suddenly erupted in New England in the most dramatic Unitarian sermon since Channing's Baltimore sermon of 1819. Parker's 1841 sermon was, like Channing's, occasioned by the ordination of a Unitarian clergyman. He borrowed the title, "The Transient and Permanent in Christianity," from an essay by D. F. Strauss.[19] Parker devoted very little attention to the permanent elements of Christianity other than defining them as "existing in the facts of human nature and the ideas of Infinite God." [20] His aim was to annihilate the transient. Traditional views of the Bible, which Parker regarded as blatant idolatry, received the brunt of his attack.

Parker began his criticisms moderately enough.

> Modern criticism is fast breaking to pieces this idol which men have made out of the scriptures. It has shown that here are the most different works thrown together; that their authors, wise as they sometimes were, pious as we feel often their spirit to have been, had only that inspiration which is common to other men equally pious and wise; that they were by no means infallible, but were mistaken in facts or in reasoning—uttered predictions which time has not fulfilled; men who in some measure partook of the darkness and limited notions of their age, and were not always above its mistakes or its corruptions.[21]

There was little here with which the traditional Unitarian scholar would disagree, and the orthodox had been confronted by these problems countless times in the past. The unreliability of the canon had been a common observation of Unitarian biblical students since the days of Buckminster. At Harvard Professor Noyes was explaining the inspiration of the prophets on the analogy of the clear truths of religion that every man receives from God. The battle of unfulfilled prophecy had been waged by him years previously, and both Norton

[19] This sermon is found in *Theodore Parker: An Anthology,* Henry Steele Commager, ed. (Boston: Beacon, 1960), p. 37. It is also known as the "South Boston" sermon, and has been widely reprinted. Page references below are taken from Commager's *Anthology.*

[20] "Transient and Permanent," p. 42.

[21] "Transient and Permanent," p. 47.

and Noyes had freely confessed the historical conditioning of the biblical writers, even that of Jesus.

As the South Boston sermon unfolded, however, it became clear that Parker intended to attack the critical assumptions of the Unitarians in much the same way in which they had so often discomfited the orthodox.

> Almost every sect that has ever been makes Christianity rest on the personal authority of Jesus, and not the immutable truth of the doctrines themselves, or the authority of God, who sent him into the world. Yet it seems difficult to conceive any reason why moral and religious truths should rest for their support on the personal authority of their revealer, any more than the truths of science on that of him who makes them known first or most clearly. It is hard to see why the great truths of Christianity rest on the personal authority of Jesus, more than the axioms of geometry rest on the personal authority of Euclid or Archimedes.[22]

This blow was aimed at the whole enterprise of Unitarian biblical studies. Since the days of Buckminster, New England liberal critics had found the center of their religious authority in the Gospel account of Jesus. They had conceived that the truths of natural religion, available to every man through his God-given reason, had been supplemented by the supernatural revelation Jesus had taught. Supernatural revelation should be received by all men, for the divinity of Jesus' message had been proven by the miracles he performed. Andrews Norton had valiantly attempted in his *Evidences of the Genuineness of the Gospels* to defend this position against the German critics. The liberals felt free to assume critical positions on other biblical problems precisely because they had been so certain of this authority.

Parker had discovered a critical vulnerability in this position. From time to time liberal critics had been forced to attribute particular ideas of Jesus' to his historical context. For instance, Jesus had believed in demons and had assumed that he was fulfilling Old Testament prophecy. Each time a concession was granted to traditional interpreters, the conservative Unitarians would assure their followers

[22] "Transient and Permanent," p. 49.

that the great truths that Jesus taught were unaffected by such historical accommodation. The circularity of such reasoning is readily apparent: some normative notion of "great truths" was being assumed by the Unitarians. Parker now made this assumption explicit. Truth may stand by itself.

> If Jesus had taught at Athens, and not at Jerusalem; if he had wrought no miracle, and none but the human nature had ever been ascribed to him; if the Old Testament had for ever perished at his birth, Christianity would still have been the word of God; it would have lost none of its truths.[23]

Parker foresaw the day when the progress of biblical criticism would make impossible any adherence to the Bible or any part of it as an infallible standard of truth. The authority of the Old Testament had already been repudiated; now the book must be accepted "for what it is worth," and read for its religion, love, and wisdom. New Testament studies were in the process of rapid change. Parker noted that one Christian writer of "unquestioned piety . . . sweeps off the beginning of Matthew. . . ."[23] That was Andrews Norton. Other critics turned their attention to John and to the Epistles. "Who shall tell us the work of retrenchment is to stop here; that others will not demonstrate . . . that errors of doctrine . . . and fact may be found . . . from the beginning of Matthew to the end of Acts?"[23] Speaking a year after he had published his review of Strauss's *Das Leben Jesu* in the *Christian Examiner,* and no longer fettered by its editorial policy, Parker intimated that the Evangelists might well have confused the actual with the imaginary and perpetrated historical and doctrinal error.

Parker's comments about the Bible were not all negative. Christianity must rely on the New Testament for "the historical statement of its facts."[24] The truths of Christianity would be true even if Jesus had been a fabrication of artful men, although had this been the case the loss of the beauty of his example to the cause of faith would be

---

[23] "Transient and Permanent," p. 50.
[24] "Transient and Permanent," p. 51.

irreparable. The whole Bible, Parker thought, revealed a "reverence for man's nature, a sublime trust in God, and a depth of piety, rarely felt in these cold northern hearts. . . ." [25] But the Bible must be the servant and not the master of Christians, and the truths it taught were to be tested "by the oracle God places in the breast." [26]

Parker's words dropped like a bomb in the midst of the New England religious dispute. The orthodox subjected the sermon to scathing scorn, calling Parker an "infidel," a "blasphemer," and a "scorner." They pointed out with self-satisfaction that Unitarianism had ended just as they had predicted: in pure naturalism. [27] Nor could the Unitarians themselves accept the sermon in good grace, although their own position of dissent made it embarrassing to attack another dissenter. Still the sermon was specifically repudiated in a number of Unitarian periodicals, and furthermore only eight Boston ministers continued to exchange pulpits with Parker. [28]

Undaunted by the uproar he had created, Parker accepted an invitation from a group of Boston laymen to lecture in the Old Masonic Temple on Tremont Street during the winter of 1841–1842. The hall, which seated 750, was filled to capacity on nearly every occasion, and the audience listened attentively to the two-hour discourses. [29] The lectures expanded on themes of the South Boston sermon and were augmented, annotated, and published in 1842 as *A Discourse on Matters Pertaining to Religion.*

Book III of the *Discourse,* "The Relation of the Religious Element to Jesus of Nazareth," reveals Parker's conversion to the critical opinions of Strauss. In the 1840 review he had criticized Strauss for assuming, without producing new evidence, that the Gospels were inauthentic. In 1842 Parker informed his audience that the date of composition, the authorship, and the historical sources of the Synoptic Gospels could not be ascertained with any certainty and that all

[25] "Transient and Permanent," p. 52.
[26] "Transient and Permanent," p. 58.
[27] See William R. Hutchinson, *The Transcendentalist Ministers* (New Haven: Yale University Press, 1959), p. 110.
[28] Hutchinson, *Transcendentalist Ministers,* pp. 110–14.
[29] Hutchinson, *Transcendentalist Ministers,* p. 115.

three represented a mixture of fact and fiction.[30] He maintained that the Gospel of John, written by an unknown author for some dogmatic purpose, had scarcely any historical value. "The author invents actions and doctrines to suit his aim, and ascribes them to Jesus with no authority. . . ."[30] In 1840 Parker had criticized Strauss's programmatic exclusion of miracles; by 1842 he could find no grounds for their support.[31] Certainly, he argued, no one aware of the principles of biblical study could use the miracles to substantiate the authority of Jesus.

Parker was willing to accept most of the destructive results of Strauss's criticism. He believed that whatever had been destroyed through biblical criticism could be reconstructed; the foundation of this belief was that there could be no doubt that the Gospels had a basis in historical fact:

> There must have been . . . a great spirit to have commenced such a movement as the Christian, a great doctrine to have accomplished this, the most profound and wondrous revolution in human affairs.[32]

As for the essence of Christianity, Parker asserted: "Whatever is consistent with Reason, Conscience, and the Religious faculty, is consistent with the Christianity of Jesus. . . ."[33] With remarkable confidence in the oracle God had placed in his soul, Parker solved a host of critical problems involved in determining the authentic words of Jesus by calmly stating, "His loftiest sayings seem to me the most likely to be genuine."[34]

In Book IV of the *Discourse,* "The Relation of the Religious Element to the Greatest of Books," Parker continued his attack on bibliolatry.

> Criticism—which the thinking character of the age demands—asks men to do consciously, and thoroughly what they have always done

[30] *A Discourse of Matters Pertaining to Religion* (4th ed.; New York: Putnam's, 1877), p. 236.
[31] *Discourse,* pp. 258, 267–68.
[32] *Discourse,* p. 233.
[33] *Discourse,* p. 271.
[34] *Discourse,* p. 234.

imperfectly and with no science but that of a pious heart; that is, to divide the word rightly; separate mythology from history, fact from fiction, what is religious and of God, from what is earthly and not of God; to take the Bible for what it is worth.[35]

And what does one do who takes the Bible for what it is worth? He makes it subservient to his soul, intellect, conscience, and affections.[36] From the strange assortment of literary forms—the fables, myths, legends, and romances—he discovers and reflects upon the lofty thoughts of nature, man, and God.[37] He studies the evolutionary progression of religious ideas from the childhood of the human race.[38] Finally, he who takes the Bible for what it is worth will find it an aid to his own God-given powers of intuition and faith, ever ready to bless, admonish, and encourage his willing heart.[39]

Parker's lectures and the publication of the *Discourse* raised a new furor among the Unitarians. Many wished to disown him entirely. His standing as a Christian minister was brought into question. Finally, the Boston Association of Ministers asked him to resign. Parker refused. He considered himself a dissenting reformer who must accomplish his task.[40]

In the *Discourse* Parker had asserted that the thinking character of the age demanded biblical criticism, demanded the thorough and scientific studies that would perform the functions formerly assumed by the pious heart: the separation of fiction from fact, of myth from history, of God's word from man's word.[41] If the age demanded criticism, Parker could supply it. If the keepers of New England theology could ignore Parker the preacher, perhaps they would hear Parker the scholar. Accordingly, in 1843, he published his translation and

[35] *Discourse*, pp. 346–47.
[36] *Discourse*, p. 305.
[37] *Discourse*, pp. 308–09.
[38] *Discourse*, p. 330.
[39] *Discourse*, pp. 353–54.
[40] Hutchinson, *Transcendentalist Ministers*, pp. 115–20. See also Perry Miller, "Theodore Parker: Apostasy within Liberalism," *Harvard Theological Review*, LIV (1961), 275–95.
[41] *Discourse*, pp. 346–47.

expansion of W. M. L. De Wette's *Critical and Historical Introduction to the Old Testament*.[42]

De Wette's *Einleitung* is recognized as the most important work of its kind to appear in the first half of the nineteenth century.[43] The author, a disciple of the neo-Kantian John Jacob Fries, synthesized the positions of Herder, Schleiermacher, and Eichhorn. A "mediating theologian," standing between the destructive naturalists and the confessed supernaturalists, De Wette considered biblical criticism to be a positive adjunct to the theology of the church. While he recognized the fundamental importance of literary criticism and pioneered in the historical criticism of the Bible, he reflected the interests of Herder in insisting that the Bible be interpreted in the religious spirit in which it had been written. The state of German critical opinion was reflected in the successive editions of De Wette's *Einleitung,* for the breadth and clarity of the work in large part depended upon the assimilation of the vast German critical literature.[44]

Parker had been interested in German biblical criticism even before entering Divinity School and soon became convinced that "Germany [was] the only land where theology was . . . studied as a science, and developed with scientific freedom." [45] De Wette's *Einleitung* represented to Parker "the most learned, the most exact, and the most critical introduction to the Old Testament ever made in any tongue. It contains the result of all the critical investigation of the human race on that subject. . . ." [46] Probably encouraged by Moses Stuart to prepare an American edition of De Wette, Parker began

---

[42] De Wette's books *Theodore; or, the Skeptic's Conversion* and *Human Life; or, Practical Ethics* had already been translated and published in the United States. On the vogue of De Wette, see Henry A. Pochman, *German Culture in America* (Madison: University of Wisconsin Press, 1961), pp. 111, 559–60.

[43] See Robert H. Pfeiffer, *Introduction to the Old Testament* (New York: Harper, 1948), p. 47.

[44] On De Wette, see Hans-Joachim Kraus, *Geschichte der historisch-kritischen Erforschung des Alten Testaments* (Neukirchen Kreis Moers: Buchhandlung des Erziehungsvereins, 1956), pp. 160–75; and T. K. Cheyne, *Founders of Old Testament Criticism* (New York: Scribner's, 1893), pp. 31–57.

[45] *Experience,* p. 59.

[46] Letter to George Ripley, 19 November 1858, in Weiss, *Parker,* I, 402.

working on the translation in 1836, shortly before assuming his duties at West Roxbury.[47] Within ten months he had completed the translation.

Parker was not content to publish a mere word for word translation of De Wette. He understood that the American popular audience, which he hoped to address, could not understand De Wette's scholarship as the learned readers of Germany could.[48] Consequently he popularized the *Introduction* by translating all De Wette's references to Latin, Greek, and Hebrew documents, and where De Wette instructed his readers to compare particular Old Testament passages, Parker printed them in full, side by side. In order to understand the state of biblical science thoroughly, Parker read all the modern introductions to the Old Testament, "from Simon down to Hengstenberg," and all the modern works he could find that related to particular critical problems. In his edition Parker added many citations of critical literature to the already copious references of De Wette, and, when he thought particular references of great importance, he translated and included such passages in the text.

To Parker the translation and expansion of De Wette represented the result "of the critical labors of the whole world upon the Scriptures," presented in a format that could be understood by an American audience.[49] He was seeking to transplant the full grown body of German biblical studies in an America where theologians had failed to grapple with the scientific spirit of the age.[50]

[47] In the translator's introduction Parker refers to an "orthodox theologian" who encouraged the project. Stuart had helped Parker in learning German (see Stanley M. Vogel, *German Literary Influences on the American Transcendentalists* [New Haven: Yale University Press, 1955], p. 26), and in view of his earlier encouragement of Everett, and for lack of knowledge of any other "orthodox theologian" who might have known of De Wette, Stuart was probably responsible for Parker's first interest.

[48] See his letter to George Ripley, 19 November 1858 in Weiss, *Parker,* I, 402–03; and *A Critical and Historical Introduction to the Canonical Scriptures of the Old Testament from the German of Wilhelm Martin Leberecht De Wette* (2 vols., Boston: Little, Brown, 1850), I, ix.

[49] *Introduction from De Wette,* I, vii.

[50] Perry Miller ("Theodore Parker: Apostasy within Liberalism") has regarded Parker's edition of De Wette as a challenge to the Unitarians, intimating that Unitarians, especially Andrews Norton, were incapable of accepting

At one time during the course of his translation Parker considered calling the work an introduction on the basis of De Wette. He had even prepared his own essays "on the credibility of the Pentateuch, on the Hebrew Prophets, on several separate books. . . ."[51] Finally, he determined to call the work a translation of De Wette's *Introduction,* both because it was a faithful translation of the whole work, and because the title seemed more modest. The essays he had prepared were excluded "for lack of space." Probably modesty and lack of space were not the only factors that influenced the final shape of the work. Parker had become a prophet without honor in his own country; he was determined that his countrymen recognize that other prophets in other lands proclaimed the same truths.[52]

Parker was willing to let De Wette's work represent the current state of scientific biblical scholarship to Americans, but he was careful that none should miss the point.

> Since the object of an introduction to the Bible is the history of the Bible, its scientific character is *historico-critical;* that is, the Bible is to be considered as an historical phenomenon, in a series with other such phenomena, and entirely subject to the laws of historical inquiry. The consideration of it in a religious view—that is, according to the dogma of inspiration and revelation—fall within the department of introduction only so far as this dogma is connected with the history of the origin of the Bible.[53]

---

negative criticism. Both Norton and George R. Noyes were as prepared to accept negative criticism of the Old Testament as Parker. Indeed in his lectures Noyes made frequent reference to De Wette. Miller says ". . . [Parker] produced a De Wette which was nothing like what the *Einleitung* dared to be in its native language." This statement certainly does not accord with Parker's statements, nor with his purpose in publishing the *Introduction.*

[51] *Introduction from De Wette,* I, x.

[52] John Edward Dirks, in *The Critical Theology of Theodore Parker* (New York: Columbia University Press, 1948), has dealt extensively with Parker's edition of De Wette and Parker as a biblical critic (pp. 33–65) but his work must be used with caution. He gives Parker credit for more originality than he deserves. For example, it was De Wette who "gave first attention to the historical formation of the canon," not Parker (p. 37). It was De Wette who "traced the Elohistic document with the help of Staehlin," not Parker (p. 38). Likewise, the quotations appearing on p. 36 are from De Wette's "Introduction," not from Parker's "Translator's Preface" (p. 10 n. 9).

[53] *Introduction from De Wette,* I, 3.

The prose was De Wette's, but Parker supplied the italics and added:

> Most of the English and American theologians . . . object to this method, and insist that the books of the Bible should be examined from a religious point of view, declaring that *dogmatic theology* is the touchstone, where with we are to decide between the true and the false. . . . [Their method] strikes a death-blow at all criticism, and commits the Bible to a blind and indiscriminating belief.[54]

Concerning the Old Testament, Parker's production was primarily aimed at the orthodox; Unitarians had long been willing to accept criticism of the Hebrew Scriptures. But Parker had served notice that he intended "at some future day, to prepare an Introduction to the New Testament, on a similar plan. . . ." [55]

It is difficult to ascertain Parker's own accomplishments as a biblical scholar from a reading of the *Introduction.* He certainly possessed the technical proficiency in languages to follow the advanced studies and demonstrated throughout a remarkable grasp of the contemporary literature on the Old Testament. When he departed from De Wette in a comment of his own, he usually delineated the mythological character of some of the narratives or claimed he had discovered the existence of documents not uncovered by De Wette.[56] In dissenting from De Wette's identification of the Elohistic source as the body of Leviticus, he anticipated the conclusions of modern scholarship that attribute the main part of the book to the Priestly source.[57] Because he accepted De Wette's revolutionary identification of Deuteronomy with the book discovered by Josiah in 621 B.C., Parker wished to date the Book of Joshua earlier than did De Wette, for he found no evidence of the Deuteronomic legislation in its narratives.[58]

Occasionally Parker added a short essay of his own to emphasize the critical conclusions of De Wette. For instance, although De Wette identified Esther as a spurious book, Parker added a long essay of his

[54] *Introduction from De Wette*, I, 4.
[55] *Introduction from De Wette*, I, x.
[56] On the Book of Judges, see *Introduction from De Wette*, II, 195–98.
[57] *Introduction from De Wette*, II, 117.
[58] *Introduction from De Wette*, II, 189.

own demonstrating the incredible aspects of the book and concluding that the whole was a "patriotic romance" without any possible recoverable historical basis.[59] De Wette had identified the characters of Nebuchadnezzar and Belshazzar in the book of Daniel as representing Antiochus Epiphanes; Parker definitely dated the composition of the book within Epiphanes' reign, and held that it was aimed at arousing patriotism and religion in the hearts of an oppressed people.[60] In a long appendix to the first volume Parker examined the canon of the Old Testament in an attempt to show that the grounds of its acceptance by Jews and Christians were so capricious that the book's religious authority could not be accepted by an rational man. Although he complained of the theological bias of many interpretations of the Old Testament, Parker disclosed his own debt to the optimistic tenor of his culture when he referred to the Old Testament as "the most valuable document for the history of human progress." [61]

Like earlier liberals who had hoped to reform New England theology with the weapons of biblical study, Parker was doomed to disappointment. His attempt to transplant comprehensive and advanced German studies by his carefully edited De Wette failed. Even the Unitarians failed to respond. Parker's disillusionment is mirrored in his letters. To De Wette he wrote in 1845:

> My translation of your work has not produced the effect here which it is yet destined to do. The Liberal party, in fact, are weak; the *so-called* Liberal party, the Unitarians are partly afraid and partly hypocritical.[62]

Thirteen years later, Parker conceded that the work had still not produced the desired effect. To George Ripley he complained: "It has never received any reasonable notice in America, for it favors the truth and not the prejudice of any sect. It has never had a friendly word said for it in any American journal." [63]

In spite of his disappointments, Parker doggedly kept the *Intro-*

[59] *Introduction from De Wette*, II, 340–45.
[60] *Introduction from De Wette*, II, 501–02.
[61] *Introduction from De Wette*, I, 21.
[62] 29 September 1845 in Weiss, *Parker*, I, 258–59.
[63] 19 November 1858 in Weiss, *Parker*, I, 402.

duction up to date, revising it as new German editions appeared. In addition to the intense personal effort required to publish the work and keep the editions current, Parker personally bore the financial expense of the project at a loss to himself. Apparently disappointment with his "labor of love" discouraged his ambitious scheme to follow the *Introduction* with a critical work on the New Testament. The last mention of that project occurs in his letter to De Wette written on 29 September 1845: "I intend . . . to prepare, with your help, a critical and historical introduction to the New Testament . . . if you prepare a new edition of your *Einleitung in das N. T.* and will send it to me. . . ." [64] Likewise, his ambition to produce a three-volume "history of the Progressive Development of Religion among the Leading Races of Mankind," failed to materialize, although Parker did make some preliminary notes on the subject.

Doubtless a great deal of Parker's interest in his ambitious projects is attributable to his fascination with languages and his admiration for scholarly studies. However, his basic aim was that the completed De Wette and the projected critical study of the New Testament and of the development of world religions should become formidable weapons in his battle with biblical authority and dogmatic theology. But Parker found that his popular writings and sermons made a greater impact on New England than did the works of critical scholarship. In matters of religion, Americans would rather depend on their pious hearts than upon scientific study.

Parker's popular writing made the Bible seem unnecessary. He spoke of the religious intuition that was possessed by every man and that afforded a direct apprehension of God, Truth, Justice, and the other virtues. And while the Bible could perform a useful function in "arousing the soul," revealing true man—"man as he should be, the divine man"—still, the Bible only "reveals to us the truths we ourselves might . . . discover at a more advanced state of progress." [65] Indeed, Parker conceived of Christianity as "the word, . . . the true Light, which has always shone, enlightening every man, so

[64] In Weiss, *Parker,* I, 159.
[65] Parker, "The Relation of the Bible to the Soul," *Western Messenger,* VIII (1840–1841), 388.

far as he was enlightened at all." [66] Such a message, so appealing to American ideas of progress and individualism, had a far more corrosive effect on New England theology than biblical scholarship.

On the surface, Parker's interest in biblical studies appears to be purely destructive. At times it seems he wished totally to depreciate the value of the Bible so that the individual soul might receive unmediated truth. Actually, however, Parker only wanted to destroy the view that gave any part of the Bible an absolute religious authority. To accomplish this purpose he marshalled all German critical artillery, even praising the destructiveness of Strauss. But Parker was not satisfied with a purely destructive view of the Bible. Like his mentor, De Wette, he wanted to see the Bible interpreted religiously and positively. The properly enlightened convert to what Parker called absolute religion could use the Bible to verify the validity of his own intuitive grasp of religious truth. Man did not stand absolutely alone before God, apprehending religious truth intuitively. Man stood within an evolutionary progressive community that included ancient Jews, Jesus, and the pious men of all times and places.

Parker concentrated his efforts on the destruction of bibliolatry. Since New England had no Strauss and no school of naturalists, he could not, like De Wette, become a mediating theologian. No one stood to his left; he was the most radical critic in America. His followers delightedly accepted his defense of the individual's intuition of religious truth, but none thought it essential to follow Parker's diligent and scholarly effort to verify that intuition by critical biblical study.

[66] Parker, "Relation of the Bible to the Soul," p. 339.

CHAPTER XI

A NEW FRONT

Josiah Willard Gibbs and Horace Bushnell on Language

T HEODORE PARKER did not wage alone his public battle against the dogmatic systems of New England theology. In Horace Bushnell, the Congregational minister of Hartford, he had a firm, if unrecognized, ally. Parker attempted to use biblical criticism as a rational weapon, seeking to demonstrate that the Bible could not serve as an authority in support of dogmatic systems. Bushnell rejected rationalism entirely and argued that language itself, especially religious or biblical language, could not bear the weight of theological systems. But nevertheless, the effect of Bushnell's position among Trinitarians resembled the effect of Parker's position among Unitarians: both tended to remove critical biblical studies from the central ground of theological and denominational debate.

Bushnell's connection with the American critical study of the Bible is slight. His writings reveal no awareness of biblical studies in Germany or of the critical opinions of American scholars. Bushnell hoped that the reform of New England theology and the reconciliation of its warring factions could be effected by a proper understanding of language. An adequate theory of language would overcome the use of biblical proof texts, rigid literalism, and the constricting creeds of dogmaticians.

In developing a theory of language that could be applied to the New England theological situation, Bushnell explicated and enlarged upon the theories of Josiah Willard Gibbs, one of his professors at the Yale Divinity School. The influence of Gibbs on Horace Bushnell has been generally overlooked by historians largely because Gibbs himself has been obscured by his more famous contemporary Nathaniel William Taylor, also on the Yale faculty, and by the notable scientific achievements of his own son, the younger Josiah Willard Gibbs.[1]

Gibbs was born in Salem, Massachusetts, in 1790. Because his father died when he was four, leaving his children to the care of their impecunious mother, the young Gibbs could not attend Harvard, where his father had graduated in 1766 and a relative, Samuel Willard, had served as acting president from 1801 to 1807. Instead Gibbs moved to New Haven to live with an uncle and attend classes at Yale, from which he graduated in 1809. From 1811 until 1815 he studied theology informally at Yale (the Divinity School was not founded until 1822) while serving as tutor at the College. Probably sometime during 1815 he moved to Andover, where he lived with the Stuart family and continued his theological studies. He did not become a candidate for the degree at Andover, but while living with the Stuarts he did study at Harvard, and received the A. M. there in 1818.[2]

Gibbs was particularly attracted to Stuart's pioneering efforts in the field of Hebrew grammar. While living with Stuart he worked on revisions of Stuart's Hebrew grammar and began the translation of Gesenius' early Hebrew lexicon. In 1824 he finished the lexicon[3] and was appointed Instructor in Sacred Languages at Yale. In 1826 he was made Professor of Sacred Literature in the new Divinity School. Gesenius published a new lexicon in 1833, and Gibbs, in

[1] However, see Roland H. Bainton, *Yale and the Ministry* (New York: Harper, 1957), p. 120; and Theodore T. Munger, *Horace Bushnell, Preacher and Theologian* (Boston: Houghton Mifflin, 1899), p. 104.

[2] On Gibbs, see Josiah W. Gibbs, *Memoir of the Gibbs Family of Warwickshire, England and United States of America* (Philadephia: Lewis and Greene, 1879); Bainton, *Yale and the Ministry,* p. 87 ff.; Muriel Rukeyser, *Willard Gibbs* (Garden City: Doubleday, 1942); Franklin Bowditch Dexter, *Biographical Sketches of the Graduates of Yale College* (New Haven: Yale, 1912), VI, 25–56; and Timothy Dwight, *Memories of Yale Life and Men* (New York: Dodd, Mead, 1903), pp. 265–77.

[3] *Hebrew and English Lexicon of the Old Testament Including the Biblical Chaldee: From the German Works of Prof. W. Gesenius* (Andover: Flagg & Gould, 1824). A second edition was published in 1832.

order to provide Americans with the best linguistic tools, began a translation of this work for publication in this country. Strangely, although both Gibbs and Robinson were Stuart's pupils, neither seemed to know of the activities of the other. Robinson completed the translation of the new lexicon and published it in 1836, at which time Gibbs had only completed about a third of the task. This was a severe disappointment to Gibbs, and clearly illustrates how far Americans were from establishing any scholarly community even within traditional confessional groups.[4]

Gibbs was a thorough and cautious scholar. During his lifetime he published very little; he left many of his articles unsigned, signed some of them with the letter "G.," and others, strangely, with "M." or "H. D. S." It almost seems that he sought obscurity. His caution in any disputed question amused his students and sometimes annoyed his colleagues. Nathaniel William Taylor, whose theology often led to heated debate, once flatly stated: "I would rather have ten settled opinions, and nine of them wrong, than to be like my brother Gibbs with none of them settled."[5] Students were fond of an anecdote relating a quarrel between Gibbs and Stuart over a vowel point in Hebrew that disappeared when one of them brushed his handkerchief across the page.[6] Even his eulogist and former pupil, George Park Fisher, felt compelled to defend Gibbs's caution.

> It was partly due to [his] uncommon candor which led him . . . to open his ear to both sides of every question. His dread of doing injustice to the advocates of an unwelcome view, may have sometimes caused him to attribute more weight to their arguments than they deserved.[7]

During the 1830's Gibbs's interests apparently began to shift from the scientific study of the Bible toward the scientific study of language. The preponderance of his published articles deal with the phenomenon of language in general as illustrated by the minute

[4] See Rukeyser, *Gibbs*, p. 51.
[5] Quoted by Bainton in *Yale and the Ministry*, p. 87.
[6] Bainton, *Yale and the Ministry*, p. 87.
[7] George Park Fisher, "Josiah Willard Gibbs," *The New Englander*, XIX (1861), 615.

and particular observations about English—"Natural Development of Anglo-Saxon English," "On the Doubling of Consonants in English"; about the classical languages—"The Crude Form of Latin Nouns," "Table of Greek Correlatives"; about the relation of European languages to Sanskrit—"View of Indo-European Cases"; or about newly discovered African languages—"A Vai Vocabulary," "A Mendi Vocabulary." [8] Lectures to his classes at the Divinity School included an emphasis on grammatical, philological, and rhetorical exegesis of Scripture.

However, Gibbs also kept abreast of trends in the critical study of the Bible. His article "Christian Theology" consisted entirely of an annotated bibliography of important works for the theological student. Gibbs's selections leaned heavily toward biblical studies and he particularly commended the most recent German works.[9] One pupil recalled Gibbs's preference for the scholarship of De Wette.[10] But it is difficult to discern Gibbs's own conclusions about the results of critical biblical study. In his published articles, and undoubtedly in his lectures as well, Gibbs carefully presented the opposing views of a number of scholars, listing the arguments for various positions. But readers or students were left to draw their own conclusions. For example, in his article "Messianic Prophecies" Gibbs surveyed a vast literature, including the views of Stuart and Hengstenberg. In concluding the article he wrote:

> Each one of these expedients or principles is perhaps possible, *per se;* many of them are plausible; all of them are not wanted or necessary; none of them, in any form yet given to them, meets the whole difficulty.[11]

Gibbs had concluded that the Pentateuch comprises several distinct documents, and he briefly discussed a few discrepancies in the

[8] Gibbs collected all his published articles and bound them in two volumes, now deposited at the Sterling Library, Yale University. The pages have been left unnumbered and subsequent references to this collection will be made by citing volume and article number.

[9] "Christian Theology," Vol. I, art. 63.

[10] Fisher, "Gibbs," p. 613.

[11] Gibbs Collection, Vol. I, art. 1.

two accounts of creation given in Genesis. To the orthodox who would deny any rift in the Mosaic unity of the books, Gibbs wrote: "It is not a question to be decided by appeals to popular impressions, but by a candid examination of all the facts." But to those who might doubt his own orthodoxy, he explained: "We believe [these apparent inconsistencies] capable of a plausible solution." While Gibbs clearly accepted a documentary hypothesis of the Pentateuch, acknowledging that some of the material did not originate with Moses, he could not entertain the conclusion that any of the material had been added after Moses. Consequently, in a view very similar to Stuart's, he held that Moses had acted as an editor of earlier material.[12]

Gibbs was also aware of certain difficulties in harmonizing the four Gospels. He wished to point out to his readers that "apparent dissonances" did not detract from the religious validity of the Gospels; he therefore cautiously presented a number of relevant considerations. Gibbs was willing to admit that the Gospels were not perfect, but hastened to add that only a theory of a God-dictated Bible made this necessary. A viable theory of revelation demanded only that the Gospels contain nothing inconsistent with religious truth. Scholars must not be alarmed to discover inconsistencies with scientific truth or dissonances arising from the remoteness of biblical culture to contemporary culture. It must be remembered that contemporary readers did not know "all the facts," and some dissonance, such as that encountered in courts of law, was to be expected, and merely authenticated the independence of the four accounts. Furthermore, a Gospel writer could not be held accountable for the statements of others which he introduced in his narrative or for the truth of documents he quoted. At this point Gibbs was willing to concede that the first chapter of Matthew might have been taken from another document and he indicated his willingness to accept this position, a position upheld by Andrews Norton in his *Genuineness of the Gospels*. Gibbs concluded in a typically cautious fashion:

[12] "Double Narrative of the Creation in Genesis," "Ante-Mosaic Origin of the Sabbath," and "Septuple Times in the Pentateuch," Gibbs Collection, Vol. II, arts. 42, 47, 48.

It is interesting and important to know that there is a life-giving power in Gospel truth, notwithstanding the apparent dissonances; that there might be a divine revelation, although the record of it were not inspired. But the sacred writers appear to claim for themselves and for each other something more than is here admitted on either of these suppositions.[13]

As cautious as Gibbs was when considering questions with theological implications, he was beginning to formulate some explicit theories of language. "Language," he wrote in 1838, "is the movement of a whole people or nation, directed by instinct, or more properly, by the laws of mind which God has constituted. . . . It is the voice of God speaking through the race." [14] Gibbs thought that scientific philology need not be dry and obscure, for it could lead directly to the discovery of metaphysical truths.

> The object of the scientific philologist is not to make distinctions, but to find them. His highest aim, his proudest triumph, is to discover the intention of the language maker. When this is done, he may be sure that he has arrived at an important and fundamental truth.[15]

Gibbs well understood, however, that grasping the intention of the "language maker" was not a simple task. In his final book, *Philological Studies,* he cautioned that all intellectual discourse is based upon the use of "faded metaphors." He explained:

> When man enters the world of intellect, there is no longer a physical relation between sounds and the ideas he may wish to communicate. Here imagination comes to his aid. Words which originally belonged to the world of sense, and denoted sensible objects, operations, and relations, are transferred, by a metaphor depending on a perceived analogy, to the world of intellect to express mental objects, operations, and relations.[16]

[13] "On the Apparent Dissonances in the Gospels," Gibbs Collection, Vol. II, art. 45.
[14] "Review of Greenlaw on the Latin Subjunctive," Gibbs Collection, Vol. I, art. 39.
[15] "View of Indo-European Cases," Gibbs Collection, Vol. I, art. 15.
[16] *Philological Studies with English Illustrations* (New Haven: Durrie and Peck, 1857), p. 15.

Gibbs pointed out that this observation could be usefully applied to biblical language and to religious controversies, and he supplied a number of illustrations. But it was Horace Bushnell who took the linguistic ideas of Gibbs and distinguished himself by applying them to the Bible and to religious language.

Bushnell was born in 1802, the son of a Connecticut farmer. He entered Yale in 1823 and graduated four years later without particular distinction. For a few years he taught school and briefly attempted a journalistic career in New York. In order to study law, he returned to Yale in 1829 as a tutor. During one of the Yale revivals he was converted, and in 1831 he entered the Divinity School. After graduating in 1833 he was ordained as the minister of the North Church in Hartford.[17]

Bushnell had already achieved some fame as a preacher and as the author of *Christian Nurture* when in 1848 the three leading theological institutions in New England—Andover, Yale, and Harvard—all invited him to deliver lectures. These three lectures were published in 1849 as *God in Christ*. In a prefatory essay, "Preliminary Dissertation on the Nature of Language," Bushnell developed a theory of language derived primarily from Gibbs, with some important influence from Coleridge. He applied this theory of language both to the Bible and to general religious discourse. The book became the center of theological controversy; Bushnell was accused of heresy and spent the next few years defending himself against this charge, bringing notoriety and fame to both himself and his theories.[18]

In the "Preliminary Dissertation" Bushnell spoke of two spheres, a lower sphere in which names were given to physical objects and simple actions, and a higher sphere of intelligent discourse available only to the "intelligent being—(*intus lego*)— . . . [a] being who

---

[17] On Bushnell, see Munger, *Bushnell; Life and Letters of Horace Bushnell*, Mary Bushnell Cheney, ed. (New York: Harper, 1860); and Barbara M. Cross, *Horace Bushnell: Minister to a Changing America* (Chicago: University of Chicago Press, 1958).

[18] *God in Christ* (New York: Scribner's, 1903). For Bushnell's most extended defense against the charge heresy, see his *Christ in Theology* (Hartford: Brown and Parsons, 1851).

can read the inner contents of words." [19] Intelligent discourse derived from a "vast analogy in things which prepares them, as forms,
to be signs or figures of thoughts, and thus bases or types of
words." [20] This "vast analogy" in turn issued from the mind of
God, who had made the universe a "vast dictionary" and a "grammar of thought." [21] Bushnell hastened to point out that words used
in the sphere of intelligent discourse could not be taken as literal
vehicles of truths, but must be accepted as hints, images, or faded
metaphors; and that understanding such discourse required "a degree of sympathy, generously extended and for a length of time,
to allow us to come into the whole or sphere of another, and feel
out . . . the real import of his words. . . ." [22]

Bushnell placed the Bible in the sphere of intelligent discourse.
He regarded the words of Scripture as the words of inspired men
striving to express their understanding of religious truth. Its language could not be accepted literally, for "there is no book in the
world that contains so many repugnances, or antagonistic forms of
assertion, as the Bible." [23] To augment the "degree of sympathy"
essential to understanding all intelligent discourse, the theologian
could turn, when interpreting the Bible, to a ". . . PERCEPTIVE
POWER in spiritual life, an unction of the Holy One, which is
itself a kind of inspiration—an immediate, experimental knowledge of God. . . ." [24] Bushnell appealed to his readers to read the
Bible with their imaginations.

> What man so-ever . . . will offer himself to the many-sided forms of
> the scripture with a perfectly ingenuous and receptive spirit . . . shall
> find his nature flooded with sense, vastnesses, and powers of truth,
> such as it is even greatness to feel. God's own lawgivers, heroes, poets,
> historians, prophets, and preachers and doers of righteousness, will
> bring him their company and representing each his own age, charac-
> ter, and mode of thought, shine upon him as so many cross lights on

[19] *God in Christ*, p. 24.
[20] *God in Christ*, p. 21.
[21] *God in Christ*, p. 22 ff.
[22] *God in Christ*, p. 48.
[23] *God in Christ*, p. 69.
[24] *God in Christ*, p. 93.

his field of knowledge, to give him the most complete and manifold view of every truth.[25]

Bushnell maintained his views of language and revelation throughout his later writings and sermons. His ideas provided a stance to criticize proof-texting theology, biblical literalism, and denominational creedalism. But in developing the linguistic ideas of Gibbs in this manner he tended to make Gibbs's biblical studies seem unnecessary: a strong dependence upon intuition, inspiration, and sympathy to interpret a biblical text made study of original languages, investigations of authorship, and historical reconstructions unimportant.

In the transition from Stuart to Gibbs and from Gibbs to Bushnell can be seen the waning interest in the critical study of the Bible. In the years following the Civil War the preacher-theologian Bushnell was to become a leading influence among Trinitarians as the preacher-theologian Parker was to become a leading influence among the Unitarians. The critical study of the Bible had been divorced from denominational and theological controversy, but no independent scholarly community existed to continue those studies.

[25] *God in Christ*, pp. 69–70.

CONCLUSION

THE strangest feature of American critical biblical studies in this early period is the fact that they vanished so quickly and made so little impact on the development of American religion after the Civil War. When Charles Briggs accepted appointment to the Edward Robinson Professorship at Union Theological Seminary in 1890 and pronounced his agreement on certain points of German higher criticism, it was generally thought that something new had been introduced to America. To be sure, the notoriety of the Briggs heresy trials brought biblical studies to the mind of the American public in an unprecedented fashion, but even the most recent historian of the Briggs affair seems to feel that Briggs was the first to introduce higher criticism to America.[1] The tradition of biblical study that flourished in New England before the Civil War has been almost entirely forgotten.

The factors leading to the sudden collapse of early critical biblical studies are not difficult to identify. The disruption created by the Civil War was of some importance. Furthermore, many of the American scholars involved in the movement died either shortly before or during the conflict—Moses Stuart and Andrews Norton in 1852, Theodore Parker in 1859, Josiah Willard Gibbs in 1861, Edward Robinson in 1863, and George R. Noyes in 1868. When these leaders died they left no successors.

Actually, American biblical studies had never been firmly established as an independent intellectual tradition. The methods, tech-

[1] Carl Eugene Hatch, *The First Heresy Trial of Charles Augustus Briggs: American Higher Criticism in the 1890's* (Ph.D. thesis, State University of New York at Buffalo, 1964).

niques, and problems of biblical study were derived from the German academic community and placed in the context of American church life. Men like Noyes and Robinson realized that Americans must find some way of sustaining the critical effort, but both fully understood the difficulties hindering the fulfillment of their hopes. The American clergy had become deeply involved in activist concerns such as the missionary societies, Bible societies, revivalism, and, above all, in New England, the anti-slavery movement. Seminaries had been charged with the task of training parish ministers whose roles had been defined by activist congregations. They could ill-afford to become too involved in purely intellectual problems. Consequently, neither the seminaries nor the clergy were able to support critical biblical scholarship on a wide scale.

That biblical studies were integrated into the seminaries rather than the universities further prevented the growth of an independent scholarly tradition. Andover, with its explicit creedalism, demanded that biblical studies be pursued only in so far as they might edify the churches and aid the progress of evangelism. In 1815 the supporters of the Harvard Divinity School asked for a separate building for divinity students, fearing that young theologians might "imbibe more of the spirit of the University than of the spirit of their profession" and come to regard their calling "as an occasion of intellectual exercise and display rather than as a means of doing good to all classes in the community." [2] The seminaries were created to serve the churches, and the churches wanted practical results.

Biblical studies in New England suffered further from their close identification with denominational and theological causes. These studies had been introduced in New England by a reforming liberal party that hoped to overthrow the hegemony of Calvinistic creedalism and to convert rational deists. But the liberals were soon identified with the distinctive doctrines of a separate Unitarian denomination. Theodore Parker subsequently attempted to use biblical criticism as a weapon of reform against conservative Unitarians and

[2] Quoted by Conrad Wright, "The Early Period (1811–1840)," in *The Harvard Divinity School,* George Huntston Williams, ed. (Boston: Beacon, 1954), p. 31.

with as little success. At the same time conservative biblical scholars had been drawn to biblical studies by the promise of defending their theology on firmer ground, buttressed by the modern critical methods of Germany. The study of the Bible never transcended these theological and denominational bounds. The circle of scholars at Harvard and the circle of scholars at Andover had little to do with one another, and even within these circles communication was poor. Furthermore, when theologies shifted from their bibliocentrism, as in the case of Parker and Bushnell, much of the impetus of biblical studies was dissipated.

Nevertheless, the critical study of the Bible in New England was an important phenomenon. In Edward Robinson it produced at least one scholar of international fame. Careful scholars such as Noyes and Gibbs might have flourished within more scholarly communities, and controversialists such as Parker, Norton, and Stuart might have become fruitful investigators had not their energies been so widely diffused. American religious life suffered a great loss with the collapse of this early movement. A necessary and useful intellectual tradition had been lost.

BIBLIOGRAPHY

BOOKS AND ARTICLES OF GENERAL SIGNIFICANCE

Barth, Karl. *Protestant Thought from Rousseau to Ritschl.* New York: Harper, 1959.

Bentley, William. *Diary.* 4 vols. Salem: Essex Institute, 1905–1914.

"Biographical Notice of the Late Samuel Dexter," *Monthly Anthology,* IX (1810), 3–7.

Bulfinch, Stephen G. "Strauss's Life of Jesus:—The Mythic Theory," *Christian Examiner,* XXXIX (1845), 145–69.

Carpenter, J. Estlin. *The Bible in the Nineteenth Century.* London: Longmans, Green, & Co., 1903.

Chable, Eugene R. *A Study of the Interpretation of the New Testament in New England Unitarianism.* Unpublished Ph.D. dissertation, Columbia University, 1955.

Cheyne, T. K. *Founders of Old Testament Criticism.* New York: Scribner's, 1893.

"Dexter Fund at Harvard University," *General Repository and Review,* I (1812), 204–09.

Eliot, Samuel A., (ed.). *Heralds of a Liberal Faith.* 3 vols. Boston: American Unitarian Association, 1910.

Ellis, George E. "The Mythical Theory Applied to the Life of Jesus," *Christian Examiner,* XLI (1846), 313–54.

Farrar, Frederick W. *History of Interpretation.* New York: Macmillan, 1886.

Faust, Clarence H. "The Background of the Unitarian Opposition to Transcendentalism," *Modern Philology,* XXXV (1938), 297–324.

Feidelson, Charles, Jr. *Symbolism and American Literature.* Chicago: University of Chicago Press, 1953.

Foster, Frank Hugh. *A Genetic History of the New England Theology.* Chicago: University of Chicago Press, 1907.

Gannett, William C. *Ezra Stiles Gannett.* Boston: Roberts, 1875.

Gatell, Frank Otto. *John Gorham Palfrey and the New England Conscience*. Cambridge: Harvard University Press, 1963.

Glover, Willis B. *Evangelical Nonconformists and Higher Criticism in the Nineteenth Century*. London: Independent Press, 1954.

Grant, Robert M. *The Bible in the Church*. New York: Macmillan, 1948.

Haroutunian, Joseph. *Piety Versus Moralism*. New York: Holt, 1932.

Harvey, Van A. "D. F. Strauss' *Life of Jesus* Revisited," *Church History,* XXX (1961), 191–211.

Herbst, Jurgen. *The German Historical School in American Scholarship*. Ithaca: Cornell, 1965.

Hitchcock, Edward. "The Connection between Geology and the Mosaic History of the Creation," *American Biblical Repository,* V (1835), 113–38, 439–51; VI (1835), 261–332.

———. "Remarks on Professor Stuart's Examination of Gen. I, in Reference to Geology," *American Biblical Repository,* VII (1836), 448–87.

Hodgson, Peter C. *The Formation of Historical Theology*. New York: Harper & Row, 1966.

Howe, M. A. DeWolfe, (ed.). *The Journal of the Proceedings of the Society Which Conducts the Monthly Anthology & Boston Review*. Boston: Boston Athenaeum, 1910.

Hutchinson, William R. *The Transcendentalist Ministers*. New Haven: Yale University Press, 1959.

Jaeck, Emma G. *Madame De Stael*. New York: Oxford, 1915.

Johnson, Robert Clyde. *Authority in Protestant Theology*. Philadelphia: Westminster, 1959.

Kraeling, Emil G. *The Old Testament Since the Reformation*. New York: Harper, 1955.

Kraus, Hans-Joachim. *Geschichte der historisch-kritischen Erforschung des Alten Testaments*. Neukirchen Kreis Moers: Buchhandlung des Erziehungsvereins, 1956.

Kümmel, Werner Georg. *Das Neue Testament: Geschichte der Erforschung Seiner Probleme*. München: Freiburg, 1958.

Long, Orie William. *Literary Pioneers*. Cambridge: Harvard University Press, 1935.

Morison, Samuel Eliot. *Three Centuries of Harvard*. Cambridge: Harvard University Press, 1936.

Morse, James King. *Jedidiah Morse, a Champion of New England Orthodoxy*. New York: Columbia University Press, 1939.

Normandie, James De. "The Manifesto Church," Massachusetts Historical Society, *Proceedings,* XLVII (1913–14), 223–31.

Palfrey, John Gorham. *Academical Lectures on the Jewish Scriptures and Antiquities.* 4 vols. Boston: James Munroe, 1838–1852.

Pfeiffer, Robert H. *Introduction to the Old Testament.* New York: Harper, 1948.

Pochman, Henry A. *German Culture in America.* Madison: University of Wisconsin Press, 1961.

Quincy, Josiah. *The History of Harvard University.* 2 vols. Boston: Crosby, Nichols, Lee, & Co., 1860.

Schweitzer, Albert. *The Quest of the Historical Jesus.* New York: Macmillan Paperbacks, 1961.

Smalley, Beryl. *The Study of the Bible in the Middle Ages.* Oxford: Clarendon Press, 1941.

Thacher, Samuel C. "Review of *The Constitution and Associate Statutes of the Theological Seminary at Andover,*" *Monthly Anthology,* V (1808), 602–14.

Vogel, Stanley M. *German Literary Influences on the American Transcendentalists.* New Haven: Yale University Press, 1955.

Willard, Sidney (trans.). "Biography of J. S. Semler," *General Repository and Review,* I (1812), 58–73, 277–96.

Willard, Sidney. *Memories of Youth and Manhood.* 2 vols. Cambridge: John Bartlett, 1855.

Williams, Daniel D. *The Andover Liberals.* New York: King's Crown Press, 1941.

Williams, George Huntston (ed.). *The Harvard Divinity School.* Boston: Beacon, 1954.

Woods, Leonard. *History of the Andover Theological Seminary.* Boston: Osgood, 1885.

Wright, Conrad. *The Beginnings of Unitarianism in America.* Boston: Starr King Press, 1955.

Wright, Conrad. "The Religion of Geology," *New England Quarterly,* XIV (1941), 335–58.

GEORGE BANCROFT

Howe, M. A. DeWolfe (ed.). *The Life and Letters of George Bancroft.* 2 vols. New York: Scribner's, 1908.

JOSEPH STEVENS BUCKMINSTER

Secondary Material

Catalogue of the Library of the Late Rev. J. S. Buckminster. Boston: John Eliot, 1812. Microfilm copy, Princeton University Library.

Lee, Eliza Buckminster. *Memoirs of Rev. Joseph Buckminster, D.D. and of His Son, Rev. Joseph Stevens Buckminster.* Boston: Ticknor, Reed, and Fields, 1851.

Norton, Andrews. "Character of Rev. Joseph Stevens Buckminster," *General Repository and Review,* II (1812), 307–14.

Ticknor, George. "Memoirs of the Buckminsters," *Christian Examiner,* XLVII (1849), 169–95.

Unpublished Material by Buckminster

Buckminster Papers. MSS, and a microfilm copy, Boston Athenaeum Library.

Books by Buckminster

Sermons, with a Memoir of His Life and Character [by S. C. Thacher]. Boston: John Eliot, 1814.

Sermons, with a Memoir of His Life and Character. 3d ed. Boston: Wells & Lilly, 1821.

Sermons, Now First Published from the Author's Manuscripts. Boston: Carter & Hendee, 1829.

Articles by Buckminster

"Abstract of Interesting Facts Relating to the New Testament," *Monthly Anthology,* V (1808), 544–47, 580–85, 633–40.

"Notice of Griesbach's Edition of the New-Testament, Now Printing at Cambridge," *Monthly Anthology,* V (1808), 18–21.

"On the Accuracy and Fidelity of Griesbach," *General Repository and Review,* I (1812), 89–101.

"Review of Dr. Miller's Retrospect of the Eighteenth Century," *Literary Miscellany,* I (1805), 82–92.

"Review of Griesbach's New Testament," *Monthly Anthology,* X (1811), 107–14, 403–21.

"Review of Sherman on the Trinity," *Monthly Anthology,* III (1806), 249–56.

"Review of *A theoretick explanation of the science of sanctity, according to reason, scripture, common sense, and the analogy of things: con-*

taining an idea of God: of his creations, and kingdoms: of the holy
scriptures: of the christian trinity, and of the gospel system, by
Thomas Fessenden," *Monthly Anthology*, II (1805), 413–28.
"Review of Thompson's Septuagint," *Monthly Anthology*, VII (1809),
396–400.
"Translation of the Article PNYMA in Schleusner's Lexicon, with
Notes," *General Repository and Review*, I (1812), 296–326.

HORACE BUSHNELL
Secondary Material
Cheney, Mary Bushnell (ed.). *Life and Letters of Horace Bushnell.* New
York: Harper, 1890.
Cross, Barbara M. *Horace Bushnell: Minister to a Changing America.*
Chicago: University of Chicago Press, 1958.
Munger, Theodore T. *Horace Bushnell, Preacher and Theologian.* Boston: Houghton Mifflin, 1899.
Smith, H. Shelton. *Horace Bushnell.* New York: Oxford, 1965.

Books by Horace Bushnell
Building Eras in Religion. New York: Scribner's, 1881.
Christ in Theology. Hartford: Brown & Parsons, 1851.
Forgiveness and Law. New York: Scribner, Armstrong, 1874.
God in Christ. New York: Scribner's, 1903.
The Vicarious Sacrifice. London: Dickinson, 1892.

WILLIAM ELLERY CHANNING
Secondary Material
Brown, Arthur W. *Always Young for Liberty.* Syracuse: Syracuse University Press, 1956.
Chadwick, John White. *William Ellery Channing.* Boston: Houghton Mifflin, 1903.
Channing, William Henry. *The Life of William Ellery Channing.* Boston: American Unitarian Association, 1896.
Review of Dr. Channing's Discourse, Preached at the Dedication of the Second Congregational Unitarian Church, New York, December 7, 1826. Boston: Hilliard, Gray, Little, & Wilkins, 1827.

Books by Channing
A Letter to the Rev. Samuel C. Thacher, on the Aspersions Contained in

a Late Number of the Panoplist, on the Ministers of Boston and the Vicinity. Boston: Wells & Lilly, 1815.

Works. Boston: American Unitarian Association, 1896.

EDWARD EVERETT

Secondary Material

Frothingham, Paul Revere. *Edward Everett*. Boston: Houghton Mifflin, 1925.

Unpublished Material by Everett

Everett Papers. MSS, Massachusetts Historical Society Library; selected portions on microfilm, Princeton University Library.

"Autobiographical Sketch of Hon. Edward Everett, May, 1838." Events up to 1819, written in another hand. With Everett Papers; microfilm copy, Princeton University Library

"Autobiography." Events up to 1814, written in Everett's hand. With Everett Papers; microfilm copy, Princeton University Library.

"Introduction to the Old Testament." MS with Everett Papers; microfilm copy, Princeton University Library.

Books by Everett

A Defence of Christianity against the Work of George B. English. Boston: Cummings & Hilliard, 1814.

JOSIAH WILLARD GIBBS

Secondary Material

Bainton, Roland H. *Yale and the Ministry*. New York: Harper, 1957, p. 87 f.

Dexter, Franklin Bowditch. *Biographical Sketches of the Graduates of Yale College*. New Haven: Yale, 1912, VI, 250–56.

Dwight, Timothy. *Memories of Yale Life and Men*. New York: Dodd, Mead, 1903, pp. 265–77.

Fisher, George Park. "Josiah Willard Gibbs," *The New Englander*, XIX (1861), 605–20.

Gibbs, Josiah W. *Memoir of the Gibbs Family of Warwickshire, England and United States of America*. Philadelphia: Lewis & Greene, 1879.

Rukeyser, Muriel. *Willard Gibbs* [Gibbs' son]. Garden City: Doubleday, 1942.

189

Books by Gibbs
Philological Studies with English Illustrations. New Haven: Durrie & Peck, 1857.

Articles by Gibbs
Gibbs Collection, published articles, collected and bound by the author in two volumes, Sterling Library, Yale University.

ANDREWS NORTON

Secondary Material
Clark, Allen S. "Andrews Norton: A Conservative Unitarian." Unpublished Honors thesis, Harvard University, 1942; microfilm copy, Princeton University Library.

Unpublished Material by Norton
Norton Papers. MSS, Houghton Library, Harvard University.
Lectures. MSS, Harvard University Archives; microfilm copy, Union Theological Seminary Library.

Books by Norton
The Evidences of the Genuineness of the Gospels. 3 vols. I, Boston: American Stationer's Company, John B. Russell, 1837; II, III, Cambridge: John Owen, 1844.
Inaugural Discourse, Delivered before the University in Cambridge, August 10, 1819. Cambridge: Hilliard & Metcalf, 1819.
Internal Evidences of the Genuineness of the Gospels. Boston: Little, Brown, 1855.
Statement of Reasons for Not Believing the Doctrines of Trinitarians Respecting the Nature of God and the Person of Christ. Boston: Wells & Lilly, 1819.

Articles by Norton
"Defence of Liberal Christianity," *General Repository and Review,* I (1812), 1–25.
"Notice of Some Publications in the Panoplist," *General Repository and Review,* II (1813), 194–223.
"On the Author of the Epistle to the Hebrews," *Christian Examiner,* IV (1827), 495–519; V (1828), 37–70; VI (1829), 198–225, 330–47.
"Review of Moses Stuart's *Letters to the Rev. Wm. E. Channing,*" *Christian Disciple,* N. S. I (1819), 316–33, 370–431.

GEORGE R. NOYES

Secondary Material

Allen, Joseph H. "George Rapall Noyes," *Christian Examiner,* LXXXV (1868), 76–81.

Kimball, John C. "George Rapall Noyes," *Heralds of a Liberal Faith,* ed. Samuel A. Eliot. Boston: American Unitarian Association, 1910, III, 269–74.

Unpublished Material by Noyes

Noyes Lectures. MSS, Harvard University Archives; microfilm copy, Princeton University Library.

Books by Noyes

An Amended Version of the Book of Job. Cambridge: Hilliard & Brown, 1827.

A New Translation of the Book of Psalms. Boston: James Munroe, 1846.

A New Translation of the Hebrew Prophets. 3 vols. Boston: James Munroe, 1837.

A New Translation of The Proverbs, Ecclesiastes, and The Canticles. Boston: James Munroe, 1846.

Articles by Noyes

"Causes of the Decline of Interest in Critical Theology," *Christian Examiner,* XLIII (1847), 325–44.

"Review of *Christology of the Old Testament,* by E. W. Hengstenberg," *Christian Examiner,* XVI (1834), 321–64.

"Stuart on the Old Testament," *Christian Examiner,* XL (1846), 69–77.

THEODORE PARKER

Secondary Material

Chadwick, John White. *Theodore Parker.* Boston: Houghton Mifflin, 1901.

Commager, Henry Steele. *Theodore Parker.* Boston: Beacon, 1947.

———. (ed.). *Theodore Parker: An Anthology.* Boston: Beacon, 1960.

Dirks, John Edward. *The Critical Theology of Theodore Parker.* New York: Columbia University Press, 1948.

Frothingham, Octavius Brooks. *Theodore Parker.* Boston: Osgood, 1874.

Miller, Perry. "Theodore Parker: Apostasy within Liberalism," *Harvard Theological Review,* LIV (1961), 275–95.

Weiss, John. *Life and Correspondence of Theodore Parker.* 2 vols. New York: Appleton, 1864.

Books by Parker

A Critical and Historical Introduction to the Canonical Scriptures of the Old Testament from the German of Wilhelm Martin Leberecht De Wette. 2 vols. Boston: Little, Brown, 1850.

A Discourse of Matters Pertaining to Religion. New York: Putnam's, 1877.

Theodore Parker's Experience as a Minister. Boston: Leighton, 1860.

Articles by Parker

"The Alleged Mistake of the Apostles," *The Scriptural Interpreter,* V (1835), 161–70.

"D. F. Strauss's Das Leben Jesu," *Christian Examiner,* XXVIII (1840), 273–316.

"How Ought the Bible to be Read?" *The Scriptural Interpreter,* VI (1836), 226–34.

"Introduction to the Second Epistle to the Thessalonians," *The Scriptural Interpreter,* VI (1836), 64–66.

"The Laws of Moses," *The Scriptural Interpreter,* VII (1837), 5–23, 60–80, 103–14, 159–78, 210–27, 258–71.

"The Relation of the Bible to the Soul," *Western Messenger,* VIII (1840–1841), 337–40, 388–96.

"Translation and Exposition of Isaiah LII.13–LIII.12," *The Scriptural Interpreter,* VI (1836), 174–90.

Material Translated by Parker

Astruc, Jean. "Conjectures upon the Original Memoirs Which Moses Made Use of to Compose the Book of Genesis," *The Scriptural Interpreter,* VI (1836), 218–26; VII (1837), 23–37, 90–94.

EDWARD ROBINSON

Secondary Material

Abel, F. M. "Edward Robinson and the Identification of Biblical Sites," *The Journal of Biblical Literature,* LVIII (1939), 365–72.

Albright, William F. "Edward Robinson," *Dictionary of American Biography.* New York: Scribner's, 1936, XVI, 39–40.

Alt, Albrecht. "Edward Robinson and the Historical Geography of Palestine," *The Journal of Biblical Literature,* LVIII (1939), 373–77.

Bewer, Julius. "Edward Robinson as a Biblical Scholar," *The Journal of Biblical Literature,* LVIII (1939), 355–63.

Smith, Henry B., and Hitchcock, Roswell D. *The Life, Writings and Character of Edward Robinson, DD., LL.D.* New York: Randolph, 1863.

Books by Robinson

The Bible and its Literature. New York: Office of the *American Biblical Repository,* 1841.

Biblical Researches in Palestine. 3 vols. Boston: Crocker & Brewster, 1874. [First published in 1841.]

Articles by Robinson

"Exodus of the Israelites out of Egypt, and Their Wanderings in the Desert," *The Biblical Repository,* II (1832), 743–97.

"Philology and Lexicography of the New Testament," *The Biblical Repository,* IV (1834), 154–82.

"Song of Deborah and Barak," *The Biblical Repository,* I (1831), 568–612.

"Theological Education in Germany," *The Biblical Repository,* I (1831), 1–51, 201–26, 409–51, 613–37.

Material translated by, edited by, or contributed to by Robinson

Buttmann, Phillipp Karl. *Buttmann's "Larger Greek Grammar": Translated from the German with Additions by Edward Robinson.* Andover: Flagg, Gould, & Newman; New York: Leavitt, 1833.

Calmet's Dictionary of the Holy Bible. Boston: Crocker & Brewster; New York: Leavitt, 1832.

"Genuineness of Isaiah, Chap. XL–LXVI, from Hengstenberg's *Christologie des Alten Testaments,*" *The Biblical Repository,* I, 700–33.

A Greek Grammar of the New Testament: Translated by Moses Stuart and Edward Robinson from the German of George Benedict Winer. Andover: Flagg & Gould, 1825.

MOSES STUART

Secondary Material

Albright, William F. "Moses Stuart," *Dictionary of American Biography.* New York: Scribner's, 1928–1944, XVIII, 174–75.

Giltner, John H. *Moses Stuart: 1780–1852.* Unpublished Ph.D. dissertation, Yale University, 1956.

Unpublished Material by Stuart

Papers. MSS, Andover Newton Theological Library; microfilm copy, Yale Divinity School Library.

Books by Moses Stuart

A Commentary on the Apocalypse. 2 vols. New York: Van Nostrand & Tervett, 1851.

A Commentary on the Book of Daniel. Boston: Crocker & Brewster, 1850.

A Commentary on the Book of Proverbs. Andover: Draper, 1870.

A Commentary on Ecclesiastes. New York: Putnam, 1851.

A Commentary on the Epistle to the Hebrews. 2 vols. Andover: Flagg & Gould, 1827, 1828.

A Commentary on the Epistle to the Romans. 4th ed., rev. by R. D. C. Robbins. Andover: Draper, 1865.

A Critical History and Defence of the Old Testament Canon. Andover: Allen, Morrill, & Wardwell, 1845.

Hints on the Interpretation of Prophecy. Andover: Allen, 1842.

Letters to the Rev. Wm. E. Channing, Containing Remarks on His Sermon Recently Preached and Published at Baltimore. Andover: Flagg & Gould, 1819.

Miscellanies. Andover: Allen, Morrill, & Wardwell, 1846.

Articles by Moses Stuart

"Are the Same Principles of Interpretation to Be Applied to the Bible as to other Books?" *American Biblical Repository,* II (1832), 124–37.

"Correspondence with Dr. Nordheimer on the Use and Omission of the Hebrew Article in Some Important Passages of Scripture," *American Biblical Repository,* XVIII (1841), 404–18.

"Creed of Arminius with a Sketch of His Life and Times," *American Biblical Repository,* I (1831), 226–308.

"Critical Examination of Some Passages in Genesis i; with Remarks on Difficulties That Attend Some of the Present Modes of Geological Reasoning," *American Biblical Repository,* VII (1836), 46–106.

"Examination of Rev. A. Barnes Remarks on Hebrews 9:16–18," *American Biblical Repository,* VIII (1842), 356–81.

"German Theological Writers," *Spirit of the Pilgrims,* I (1828), 164–68.

"Have the Sacred Writers Anywhere Asserted That the Sin or Righteousness of One is Imputed to Another?" *American Biblical Repository,* VII (1836), 241–330.

"Hebrew Lexicography," *American Biblical Repository,* VIII (1836), 448–94.

"Hints Respecting Commentaries upon the Scriptures," *American Biblical Repository*, III (1833), 130–85.

"How Are the Designations of Time in the Apocalypse to be Understood?" *American Biblical Repository*, V (1835), 33–83.

"Interpretation of Psalm XVI," *American Biblical Repository*, I (1831), 76–110.

"Interpretation of Romans 8:18–25," *American Biblical Repository*, I (1831), 363–406.

"Is the Manner of Christian Baptism Prescribed in the New Testament?" *American Biblical Repository*, III (1833), 288–390.

"Meaning of *Kyrios* in the New Testament, Particularly as Employed by Paul," *American Biblical Repository*, I (1831), 733–75.

"On the Alleged Obscurity of Prophecy," *American Biblical Repository*, II (1832), 216–45.

"On the Meaning of the Word *pleroma* in the New Testament; and particularly on the Meaning of the Passage in which it Occurs in Col. 2:9," *American Biblical Repository*, VIII (1836), 373–428.

"On the Study of the German Language," *Christian Review*, VI (1841), 446–71.

"Remarks on the Internal Evidence Respecting the Various Readings in 1 Tim. 3:16," *American Biblical Repository*, II (1832), 57–79.

"Remarks on Jahn's Definition of Interpretation and Some Topics Connected with It," *American Biblical Repository*, I (1831), 135–59.

"Review of *The Evidences of the Genuineness of the Gospels*, by Andrews Norton," *American Biblical Repository*, XI (1838), 265–343.

"Samaritan Pentateuch and Literature," *American Biblical Repository*, II (1832), 681–723.

Grammars by Stuart

A Grammar of the New Testament Dialect. Andover: Gould & Newman, 1834.

A Hebrew Chrestomathy, Designed as an Introduction to a Course of Hebrew Study. 2d ed. Andover: Flagg & Gould; New York: Leavitt, 1832.

A Hebrew Grammar with a Copious Syntax and Praxis. Andover: Flagg & Gould, 1821.

A Hebrew Grammar with a Praxis on Select Portions of Genesis and the Psalms. Andover: Flagg & Gould, 1823.

A Hebrew Grammar without the Points; Designed as an Introduction to the Knowledge of the Inflections and Idiom of the Hebrew Tongue. Andover, 1813.

Material translated by, edited by, or contributed to by Stuart

"Commentary on Isaiah 17:12–14, 18:1–7. Translated from the German of Gesenius by Prof. Wm. S. Tyler, with Remarks by Prof. Stuart," *American Biblical Repository,* VIII (1836), 195–220.

Elements of Interpretation, Translated from the Latin of J. A. Ernesti, and Accompanied by Notes and an Appendix Containing Extracts from Morus, Beck and Keil. Andover: Mark Newman, 1827.

"Exegesis of Isaiah XV. XVI. Translated from the German of Gesenius, by W. S. Tyler, Theol. Sem. Andover; with Remarks and Notes by M. Stuart," *American Biblical Repository,* VII (1836), 107–60.

A Greek Grammar of the New Testament: Translated by Moses Stuart and Edward Robinson from the German of George Benedict Winer. Andover: Flagg & Gould, 1825.

Hebrew Grammar of Gesenius as Edited by Roediger, Translated, with Additions and Also a Hebrew Chrestomathy. Andover: Allen, Morrill, & Wardwell, 1846.

"On the Use of the Particle *hina* in the New Testament, Translated from the Latin of Professor Tittmann of Leipsic, with Notes," *American Biblical Repository,* V (1835), 84–112.

"What Has Paul Taught Respecting the Obedience of Christ? Translated from the Latin of Tittmann, with Notes and Remarks," *American Biblical Repository,* VIII (1836), 1–87.

INDEX